FROM DUCK SOUP
TO CHICKEN WITH CASHEW NUTS

From Canton—Lemon Chicken and Braised Drumsticks in Curry Sauce.

From Fukien—Fried Duck with Fermented Red Wine Lees Paste and Braised Chicken Breast with Scallions.

From Hunan—Stir-Fried Spicy Chicken Livers with Leeks and Cold Chicken with Chili Pepper Oil Sauce.

From Peking—Velvet Chicken and the legendary Peking Duck.

From Shanghai—Beggar's Chicken and Drunken Chicken.

From Szechuan—Eight Precious Duck and Fried Chicken with Szechuan Peppercorn Sauce.

From all over China come hundreds of delicious reasons why a bird in a Chinese chef's hands leads to the most marvelous and varied creations ever to grace a dining table.

CHINESE POULTRY COOKING

ABOUT THE AUTHOR: STELLA LAU FESSLER was born in Hong Kong, where she studied Chinese cooking for several years in a school for professional cooks, as she later was to study French cuisine in Paris. Currently she divides her time between lecturing in Chinese at Cornell University and conducting a near-legendary course in Chinese cooking in her own home. Ms. Fessler is the author of *Chinese Meatless Cooking* and *Chinese Seafood Cooking*, also available in Plume editions.

CHINESE POULTRY COOKING

STELLA LAU FESSLER

ILLUSTRATED BY JANET NELSON

A PLUME BOOK

NEW AMERICAN LIBRARY

TIMES MIRROR

NEW YORK AND SCARBOROUGH, ONTARIO

NAL BOOKS ARE AVAILABLE AT QUANTITY DISCOUNTS WHEN USED TO PROMOTE PRODUCTS OR SERVICES. FOR INFORMATION PLEASE WRITE TO PREMIUM MARKETING DIVISION, THE NEW AMERICAN LIBRARY, INC., 1633 BROADWAY, NEW YORK, NEW YORK 10019.

PLUME TRADEMARK REG. U.S. PAT. OFF. AND FOREIGN COUNTRIES REGISTERED TRADEMARK—MARCA REGISTRADA. HECHO EN HARRISONBURG, VA., U.S.A.

SIGNET, SIGNET CLASSICS, MENTOR, PLUME, MERIDIAN and NAL BOOKS are published in the United States by The New American Library, Inc., 1633 Broadway, New York, New York 10019, in Canada by The New American Library of Canada, Limited, 81 Mack Avenue, Scarborough, Ontario M1L 1M8.

Library of Congress Cataloging in Publication Data

Fessler, Stella Lau.
    Chinese poultry cooking.

    Includes index.
    1. Cookery (Poultry)   2. Cookery, Chinese.
I. Title.
TX750.F47   1982   641.6′65   82-12420
ISBN 0-452-25365-9

First Printing, November, 1982

1 2 3 4 5 6 7 8 9

PRINTED IN THE UNITED STATES OF AMERICA

CONTENTS

ACKNOWLEDGMENTS

Since a book like this must be based on the efforts of generations of chefs, I would like to acknowledge my debt to the rich heritage of Chinese cuisine and all the cooks, known or unknown, throughout Chinese history for their imaginative inventions and delightful contributions to the culinary art of China.

My sincere thanks to Mr. David Chang, my colleague at Cornell University for his invaluable help on botanical identifications of many spices used in this book.

I would like to express my deepest gratitude to my editor Carole Hall and to Veronica Johnson for their painstaking attention to detail; their efforts have improved my book considerably.

Finally, my appreciation to Cornell University for providing the research facilities and the congenial environment that made it easier and more pleasurable to write this book.

CHINESE POULTRY COOKING

INTRODUCTION

If there is ever a poultry-cooking contest among all the nations in the world, I think China would very likely win the prize for having the greatest diversity of poultry dishes. The list is endless: chicken, duck, goose, squab, sparrow—boned, whole, sliced, braised, poached, stir-fried, in Peking, Shanghai, Cantonese, Szechuan, Fukien, or Hunan style. In addition to using the meat portion of a bird, the Chinese make intricate, robust banquet dishes out of parts considered inferior by American standards, such as the innards, feet, wings, and even the blood.

In Chinese culture, birds—big and small, domestic or wild—have always been looked upon as ingredients for the festive board. A Chinese family, however poor it might be, must have at the minimum a chicken or a duck on the table at any celebration. The better-off families, it goes without saying, often will present an array of exotic dishes of various fowl. It is believed that the richer the display and diversity of food on a convivial table, the greater the fortune to follow. In the old days, however, chicken brought bad luck to some Chinese. During a traditional company New Year's Eve banquet, when an employer wanted to sack someone, he did not have to face the uneasy and uncomfortable situation of having to tell his man so. He would simply point the chicken head directly at the employee and that man would know he was no longer needed.

Of all the birds that the Chinese use to grace their dinner tables, chicken and duck are the most common. Between the two, chicken provides the greater number of cooking variations. One chicken can be used for many dishes; the white meat for stir-frying, dark meat for braising or steaming, giblets for deep-frying or stir-frying with vegetables, the blood for making pudding and adding to soup, the intestines either for red-cooking or making broth in the same pot with the feet and the neck. Chicken broth, regarded as an elixir, is often steamed with medicinal herbs to brew a rich tonic for the sick, the weak, and the elderly. Chicken fat is rendered and used for stir-frying with vegetables. The feathers are gathered and sent to small handicraft shops for making toys and beautiful feather dusters.

In the past, chicken was served only at festivals and on special occasions. Today, with new techniques of raising fowl, chicken is readily available at a very reasonable price. This enables us to maintain our good health while fighting inflation as well.

Because chicken can be raised easily with very little care, it is a popular food. Most Chinese living in rural areas have chickens running around in their courtyards. Many urban dwellers in Macau and Hong Kong also raise a few chickens on their rooftops and balconies. Chicken occupies a high place in Chinese culinary arts.

One should keep in mind that in China cooks use different sizes of chicken to prepare different dishes, and purchases should be made accordingly. A young bird, such as a fryer or a broiler of 2 to 3 pounds, is good for steaming, poaching, and stir-frying; a roasting chicken weighing 4 to 6 pounds is for braising with soy sauce; Rock Cornish game hen is excellent for deep-frying; stewing chicken would be used for making soups only. In writing this book, I have experimented and have called for the most appropriate age and weight of the bird for each of the dishes. When following the recipes in this book, if you use the type of chicken specified for the dish and the proper cooking time you will certainly get the best results.

Duck is almost as versatile as chicken in the world of Chinese cooking. Duck feet, gizzards, tongues, and brains are considered items of great delicacy. Some Chinese will fight a hard battle at the table to get the duck tail. In China, ducks symbolize fidelity because they often swim in pairs.

There are two kinds of ducks used in Chinese cooking. One is the famous white-feathered Peking duck, the ancestor of the Long Island duck, which was imported to America in 1873. Since Peking ducks are raised in confinement and force-fed with a mixture of carbohydrate-rich grains, they are larger and have very tender meat. The other variety is farm duck or shore duck. This species possesses grayish feathers and is a leaner duck, excellent for braising and stewing. They are reared by being allowed to roam freely around the farmyard and along the shores of rivers and lakes. Because of the exercise they get, their meat is slightly tougher than that of Peking ducks, but the flavor is tastier. These ducks are more widely used and more favored than the fat Peking duck, and most Chinese duck dishes are made from them.

Chinese ducks are cooked whole—roasted, braised, smoked, stuffed, or stewed. Very few dishes are done with boned duck meat. Usually a prepared duck is cut up into bite-sized pieces and served to as many as ten people, unlike Western dining where one duck is only sufficient for two.

The less frequently used but highly prized party birds are goose, squab, pheasant, quail, and rice sparrow. These delicacies are relished most by Southern Chinese. In this book I have included a few delicious and easy to prepare recipes for these birds. Squab and quail, when unavailable, can be replaced with Rock Cornish game hen. Although turkey and capon are not a traditional part of Chinese menus, a great number of Chinese like myself have discovered, through years of experiment, that when prepared in a Chinese manner, these large birds are just as scrumptious as the smaller ones. In fact I think a small smoked turkey surpasses a traditional smoked chicken. The bulk of an 8-to-10-pound turkey retains its juice better, hence it is moister and much more tender. Today, with turkey being sold all year round, it is an economical meat for delightful dining on any occasion. In recipes in this book, whenever suitable, I have inserted turkey or capon as an alternative. The popularity of incorporating these birds into Chinese cooking is growing.

The dishes in this book are drawn from all over China, giving you a solid repertoire of poultry dishes from many cuisines across hundreds of years. The techniques are very basic and useful for both Chinese-style or Western-style cooking. The recipes are divided into six distinctive regions: Canton and South China; Fukien and Taiwan; Hunan; Peking and Northeast China; Shanghai and East-Central China; Szechuan and West-Central China. Except for Hunan, two to five provinces are grouped into one region according to the similarity of their cooking styles.

BASICS OF
CHINESE POULTRY
COOKING

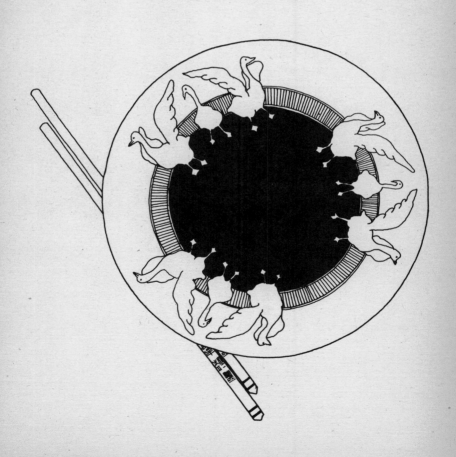

HOW TO SELECT POULTRY

Except for the packaged frozen American chicken sold in Hong Kong markets, I have seen only live or fresh-killed chicken or ducks in China, Taiwan, Hong Kong, and Macau. Since the Chinese are so mindful of flavors in everything they eat, they prefer to buy their birds live and have the butcher kill and clean them while they keep their watchful eyes on the entire process. They know that only fresh-killed poultry has the best taste.

When the Chinese shop for a chicken for their dinner, they follow a fascinating set of rituals. First, they tell the butcher the size of bird that they want to buy. The butcher then picks out one among a flock of about fifty. With one hand he grasps the chicken wings and bends them together toward the back. The bird is turned over with the breast side facing upward. The buyer will then proceed to examine the fowl by feeling the meat around the breast to check if it is plump and soft. He also gently pushes down the tip of the breastbone; if it is flexible, the chicken is a young one. Next, he will blow the feathers apart to look at the skin; young chickens have smooth skin with tight, small pores, but on older ones the skin is loose with larger pores. If the buyer is not satisfied with the bird, this routine will be repeated over and over again. I have played the same game innumerable times too, and I must confess that the chicken I ended up buying was not always the best of all the birds that the butcher so patiently displayed. However, nobody feels secure making the decision on the very first fowl that the butcher picks out and must check at least five to ten of them.

In the West, buying live chicken is a rarity. Most birds we buy are already cleaned and packed for the supermarkets. I suppose this is much more convenient for our busy lives, even if it means we have to forego a little bit of the taste. But when buying a whole chicken or the cut-up parts, always try to buy on the day you are going to cook or no more than one day beforehand. Cleaned fowl deteriorates much faster than red meat and should not be kept in the refrigerator unfrozen longer than two days. The fresher the poultry, the tastier it is. There is positively an extra sweet taste in a freshly killed fowl. If you shop at a particular supermarket all the time, find out what day of the week the chickens are delivered so you will know just how long they have been stored in the chiller. Or read the date on the label and inspect the meat carefully. On fresh-killed poultry the skin is smooth and the meat is very firm. If the package is full of water, the chicken very likely has been frozen and defrosted, in which case you should not buy it. Frozen chicken loses much of its flavor and the meat tends to be drier and coarser. When possible, use chicken that has never been frozen.

Almost all ducks, geese, turkeys, capons, and Rock Cornish game hens are sold frozen. However, if you live near a farm, sometimes fresh-killed ducks, geese, and turkeys are available, especially around Thanksgiving and Christmas. Butchers in larger Chinatowns also sell unfrozen ducks, squabs, and geese.

HOW TO KILL AND CLEAN POULTRY

Today, few people in the United States actually have to kill and clean live poultry themselves. I am sure most of you will not need this section at all. Nevertheless, if you are adventurous, this part may come in handy. The following instructions describe the Chinese way of slaughtering chickens, ducks, and other smaller birds.

Pull the wings back and grasp them with the left hand, leaving the little finger free. With the right hand bend the neck straight backward toward the wings and insert the nape of the neck skin tightly between the thumb and the index finger that are holding the wings. Next use the right hand to pick up the left foot and hook it onto the little finger of your left hand. This will prevent the bird from kicking. Next, holding a sharp knife in your right hand, cut the throat about 1 inch below the head. Quickly turn the bird over and drain out the blood. (Left-handed people can change hands in these instructions.) Place the bird in a large basket or a bucket until it is completely quiet. In a large kettle heat 3 to 4 gallons of water to 60°C. or 140°F. Put the bird into the hot water and soak for 6 to 10 minutes. Turn the bird over a few times with a long wooden spoon. Remove bird from the hot water and place it on the drain board. Then pull the layers of thick skin from the feet and the plastic-like cover from the beak. Next remove feathers by plucking them in the same direction they have grown. If the feathers don't come off easily, dip the fowl into the hot water for a few more minutes. Very fine and downy feathers are easier to remove with tweezers or by singeing them over a low flame.

Lay the bird on its back. With a knife or a pair of scissors make a 2-inch cut from the tail up toward the center of the breast-bone. Insert your hand into the opening, loosen the intestines, and take out the innards and the esophagus. Rinse the cavity thoroughly and drain. The bird is now ready for cooking.

Separate the heart, liver, and gizzard. Remove the fat on the gizzard, then split it open crosswise along the curve. Turn the gizzard inside out, empty and discard everything inside the gizzard, peel off and discard the yellow inner lining. Rub the gizzard with 1 teaspoonful of salt and rinse thoroughly. Cut and discard the greenish gallbladder from the liver, taking care not to break it, then trim off the tough membrane attached to the liver. Remove arteries and blood from the heart. Rinse the giblets and drain.

HOW TO BONE POULTRY WHOLE

The versatility of a boned bird is immense. It can be used for Chinese-style or Western-style dishes depending upon the fillings stuffed into the cavity, and all the work of boning, stuffing, and cooking can be done hours or even days in advance. The art of boning a bird is relatively easy to master; once you understand the procedure and acquire the skill, it takes only a few minutes. Once in the People's Republic of China at the Ding Shan Hotel in Nanking, I saw three young chefs taking a test for promotion to a more senior position. The task for each of them was to bone three things: a chicken, a whole pork loin, and a fish. The fastest one took less than two minutes to bone the chicken.

The following instructions can be applied to birds of all sizes. These boning techniques keep the whole bird intact and little trussing is required after it has been stuffed.

To bone a bird, start from the neck and work toward the tail. First, pull back the neck skin and turn it inside out as far back as possible over the shoulders. With a very sharp pointed knife, cut free the meat surrounding the wishbone, the collarbones, and the shoulder blades. Disjoint these bones and discard them, leaving the wings unboned. The wings should now be completely separated from the main carcass. Snip and scrape the flesh around and away from the skeleton. Always direct the edges of the blade against the carcass as close as possible so that you are actually scraping the meat away from the bones. Continue cutting loose the meat around the spine and the breast. Fold the loose meat and skin inside out and pull it down further toward the legs, like rolling down a stocking. Take special care when separating the white meat from the ridge of the breastbone. Do not slit or puncture the skin. Cut through the joints attaching the thighbones to the backbone. Cut and scrape to free the meat around the thighbone. When you arrive at the ball joints of the thigh and the drumstick, cut and separate the thighbone from the drumstick. Discard the thighbone, but leave the drumstick unboned and attached to the meat. Repeat the procedure with the other leg. Lift up the entire skeleton and cut loose the backbone from the tail, leaving the tail connected to the meat and skin. Save the skeleton for soup stock. Turn the whole bird skin-side out into its original shape. The bird is now ready for stuffing.

HOW TO CUT RAW POULTRY INTO SERVING PIECES

Since the Chinese use chopsticks as their eating implements, poultry is cut up into smaller portions than it might be for a Western dish. Raw poultry generally is cut into slightly large chunks than cooked, because after it has been cooked the pieces shrink.

Cutting up a raw bird is quite simple. The first step is to find where all the joints are located, then learn to disjoint each piece properly. The next step is to cut the sections into small chunks. All birds possess the same basic anatomy; so it is worthwhile to master this skill in order to cut up birds of all sizes. A heavy Chinese cleaver and a thick chopping board are all that is needed.

Place the poultry on the chopping board with the breast facing up. Disjoint and remove the wings from the body by separating them from the shoulder joints. Cut each wing crosswise in two at the middle joint, leaving the tip of the wing attached. Snip off the legs (thigh and drumstick) at the joint between the backbone and the thighbone. Cut each thigh and drumstick apart through the joint. With the cleaver, chop each thigh crosswise, bone and meat, into two or three equal portions depending on the size of the bird; chop each drumstick crosswise in the same fashion into two or three sections. Split the body of the bird lengthwise in two by cutting down through the breastbone and the backbone. Chop each half of the breast meat and backbone crosswise into pieces 1½ inches wide.

HOW TO CARVE COOKED POULTRY CHINESE FASHION

Apart from a few minor variations, carving a cooked bird is almost the same as cutting up a raw one. After a cooked bird has been cut up, the pieces are always neatly assembled on a serving platter to reconstruct its original figure. Again, you need a heavy Chinese cleaver and a thick chopping board.

Disjoint the bird according to the instructions given for cutting up raw poultry, but after separating the wings, the thighs, and the drumsticks, do not cut those pieces immediately; set them aside. Divide the breast and the backbone by cutting down through the rib bones on both sides. Pile the pieces at one corner of the board or remove them. Place the strip of backbone on the chopping board, skin-side up, then chop it crosswise into pieces 1 inch wide. Place the palm of your left hand on top of the pieces of bird. With your right hand hold the broad blade of the cleaver parallel to the chopping board, insert the blade under the pieces of food, scoop them up, and slide them onto a plate without disturbing the shape. Split the breast lengthwise into two halves; with skin-side up cut each half crosswise into 1-inch-wide pieces. Applying the same method as above, transport and place half of the breast on the plate at the left side of the backbone and the other half on the right side. Chop the thighs and drumsticks across the bones into 1-inch-wide pieces, also with the skin facing up. Place one thigh next to the lower part of the breast meat on each side of the plate; arrange and attach the drumsticks to the thighs. Separate the wings at the joints and lay them on the upper corner at each side of the plate next to the breast meat with their tips turning outward.

The arrangement on the plate is supposed to look like the bird has been flattened totally with each part still in its original position. If the instructions seem too complicated, just cut up the bird into bite-sized pieces and enjoy the dish.

HOW TO BONE COOKED POULTRY

A cooked bird or cooked poultry legs and breast are very easy to bone. It is important to allow the meat to become completely cool and the juices to soak back into the meat before removing the bones.

With a knife or a cleaver, disjoint the wings and legs as instructed on page 13 (How to Carve Cooked Poultry Chinese Fashion). Put a leg on the carving board, skin-side down. With a sharp knife, make an incision lengthwise along the natural line of the thighbone and drumstick bone. Dig in with your finger and lift and pull away the thighbone and drumstick bone. Handle them carefully and try not to tear apart too much meat. After the bones are removed the leg should still be intact and in its original shape. Strip the meat from the wings and discard the bones. Place the body of the bird on the board, with breast-side up; insert one hand into the tail opening and press down on the backbone. With the other hand in the same opening, pull up the whole breast and tear the body apart, separating the breast and backbone. Remove meat from backbone and discard the whole spine. Turn the breast upside down. With each hand grasping onto each side of the breast, bend the two sides backward firmly until the breastbone snaps open. Remove rib bones and free the white meat from the breastbone.

Cooked poultry pieces are boned according to the instructions for whole poultry above.

HANDLING CHICKEN BREAST

Of all the birds and the various parts of their bodies used in Chinese poultry cooking, chicken breast is the most versatile. Since the breast meat is the tenderest of it all, it is generally used for quick stir-fried dishes. The meat is either diced, sliced, shredded, or pureed and cooked with vegetables or nuts to give the dish color, flavor, texture, and contrast.

BONING CHICKEN BREAST

There are many ways of boning a raw chicken breast; the following method is one version. First, pull off the skin, working from the top down toward the tip of the breastbone. With a sharp knife, starting from the center, cut loose the meat along the ridgebone on one side of the breast. As you cut, lift and pull the loose flesh away from the bone. Aim the blade close to the bone at all times and work from the center toward the side. Cut and scrape to free the meat from the breastbone and the ribs. Repeat the same method and free the meat on the other side.

SLICING CHICKEN BREAST

Trim off fat and membrane from the breast meat; separate two strips of fillet from the main parts. Place one section of meat at a time flat on the cutting board, pressing down lightly with the palm and the fingers of the left hand on top of the part that is being cut; be sure to turn the tips of the fingers slightly upward. With the right hand hold the cleaver parallel to the cutting board; cut and slice the meat into thin pieces about ⅛-inch thick by sawing with the blade. Repeat with the rest of the meat.

CUTTING CHICKEN BREAST INTO THIN SLIVERS

First, slice the breast into thin pieces according to the instructions above, then cut the slices along the grain into strips. Stack two to three slices together. Cup the left hand and put it palm down on the meat with the fingernails lined up straight along the line to be cut. The knuckles will now form a vertical wall against which to place the flat blade of the cleaver. Grasp the cleaver with your right hand and place the flat blade against the knuckles of the left hand. The knuckles should always touch the side of the flat blade to serve as a cutting guide. Now cut straight down, and matchstick-sized thin strips will be produced. For this kind of cutting, it is best to start down with the front end of the blade, which is the end farthest away from you. Simultaneously press the knife downward and away from your body. By the time the entire length of the blade has glided through the meat, the strips should be formed. After completing this motion, the curved fingers of the left hand move backward a little from the edge of the meat, exposing a new area for cutting. The thickness of the strips is determined by how far back the fingers move from the edge.

DICING CHICKEN BREAST

Cut breast meat into strips about ⅓-inch wide. Gather a few strips and lay them parallel to each other, then cut them cross-wise into ⅓-inch squares. When diced chicken is to be cooked with ingredients that are bigger than ⅓-inch square, slice the strips thicker and enlarge the squares as well.

PUREEING CHICKEN BREAST

There are two methods of pureeing chicken breast. One is the traditional Chinese way, which is manual; the other way is to use a food processor. Both techniques are included here.

Traditional method: Remove skin and separate the fillets. Lay one strip of breast meat at a time on a cutting board, with the side next to the skin facing down. Holding one end of the strip with one hand, with the other hand scrape the meat with the tip of the blade of a sharp knife. As you scrape, the meat turns into a paste, leaving the membrane and the stringy white tendon on the board. Discard membrane and tendon; repeat with the rest of the breast. Chop the scraped meat until it is very fine. As you chop, add about 4 tablespoonsful of chicken stock to the meat a little at a time, flipping and chopping until the stock is completely absorbed into the meat and the paste becomes fluffy.

Using a food processor: Scrape the chicken as instructed above. Using the metal blade, in the beaker or the bowl of the processor combine the scraped chicken with ⅓ cup chicken stock and process until the mixture is smooth and creamy. This can also be done in a blender.

POACHING

Poaching is the simplest and easiest way of cooking fowl. It requires neither preliminary preparation nor constant attention when it is on the stove. The bird practically cooks itself. Generally, younger birds are used in poaching for Chinese dishes. If a chicken is to be poached, pick a fryer or a broiler.

The actual cooking time is much shorter than poaching the Western way. The Chinese prefer their poultry just nicely cooked through with the marrow in the bones still red. A 3-pound chicken should be cooked for only 30 minutes and soaked for 1 more hour to let the residual heat of the hot water do the remainder of the cooking. This way the bird is never overcooked and the meat is moist and tender. For those who like their meat well done, add 5 to 10 minutes to the cooking time.

Use a pot not too much larger than the bird, which will hold it just snugly but with enough space on top so that when the bird is put inside, it will be completely submerged in water. Test the bird in the pot before you start poaching. Fill the pot with water to cover the entire bird, add 3 slices of fresh ginger, 3 whole scallions, and 1 tablespoonful of Chinese rice wine, sake, or dry sherry. Bring the water to a boil over high heat, and immerse the bird. The temperature of the liquid will drop when the poultry is added, so continue to heat the liquid over high heat until the water is about to simmer; do not allow the liquid to come to a rolling boil. Cover the pan and regulate the heat. Cook for 30 minutes.

Be sure to keep the water just below the boiling point throughout the entire cooking time. There should be only a few small bubbles floating on the surface of the water. Turn off the heat and let the bird soak in the hot liquid for 1 hour. Since the cooking time is relatively short and the water is never allowed to boil, the stock in the pot does not really have much taste at all. It is quite justifiable to discard it or, if you wish, to use it as a weak soup base. Cut-up large-sized poultry pieces can be poached in the same manner, but reduce the liquid and the cooking time.

POACHING POULTRY IN MASTER SAUCE

Master sauce is a rich marinade of soy sauce, rice wine, sugar, and many spices. It is the hallmark of Southern Chinese cooking. Duck, chicken, goose, squab, and sparrow are popular poultry to prepare with master sauce. Once the first batch of sauce is made it becomes somewhat immortal. The stock is used over and over again with fresh soy sauce, wine, and spices added whenever the aromatic flavor becomes bland. The sauce is enriched and becomes stronger and stronger with each additional cooking of poultry. Restaurants sometimes are judged by the tastiness of their master sauce. In restaurants, the sauce is used continuously day after day and year after year, so there is no time for the stock to become spoiled. At home, after each use store the stock in a plastic container and keep frozen until needed.

Cooking poultry in master sauce is similar to poaching a bird in water, only the liquid has been flavored. For every 2 cups of water add 1½ cups soy sauce, ½ cup Shao-sing rice wine, sake, or dry sherry, ½ cup rock candy or brown sugar, 4 slices of fresh ginger, 1 tsp Szechuan peppercorns, 1 tsp fennel seeds, 2 whole star anise, 8 cloves, 2 nutmegs, 1 cinnamon stick, and 6 slices of licorice root about ½ inch in diameter. (Licorice root can be omitted if it is unavailable.) Combine all the ingredients in a heavy pot and bring to a boil, then cover and simmer over a low fire for 20 minutes. The master sauce can be prepared ahead of time and kept in the refrigerator or the freezer. Poach and soak the poultry according to instructions given in each individual recipe using the same method as poaching a bird in water.

SMOKING

Smoking is another technique commonly used in flavoring Chinese poultry dishes, particularly those that are from Szechuan and Hunan provinces. Almost every type and any size of bird are suitable for smoking. Smoking also serves as a means of preserving the food.

There are two Chinese smoking methods. One is quite similar to the Western method. The pieces of meat or fowl to be smoked are placed on a rack inside a large container, beneath which is a small clay burner containing hot charcoal, flavored sawdust, and tea leaves or spices. The entire apparatus is then covered tightly in order to allow the smoke to permeate the food.

The other method is to heat brown sugar, rice, and spices in a pan or a wok to create the smoke. To use this method, line a large old wok, a dutch oven, or a roasting pan with aluminum foil, and spread the amount of rice, brown sugar, and spices specified in the recipe you are following evenly in the center part, in approximately the same diameter as your burner. Place a cake rack or roasting rack over this, and on the rack place the poultry or meat to be smoked. Cover the pan tightly and seal the seams with damp paper towels or wet rags. Set the pan over medium heat and smoke. To prevent getting a bitter taste, rotate the pan from time to time so that new areas will be burned in order to generate fresh smoke. I recommend removing the lid outdoors to spare your kitchen the heavy smoke.

STIR-FRYING POULTRY MEAT

Poultry meat cut up into small morsels, thin strips, or diced cubes is first flavored with wine and salt and then coated with cornstarch and egg white to seal the pieces before cooking. This step gives a smooth texture to the outside of each piece of meat and prevents the flavor and juices from escaping. The meat is then cooked in a generous amount of hot oil very quickly and, when done, is removed from the oil and drained. Later the poultry pieces are returned to the pan and stirred with vegetables or other accompanying ingredients, then glazed with a sauce.

In general, all the components that go into the same dish should be cut in uniform size and shaped to conform to the principal ingredient of the dish. If the meat is cut into small cubes the accompanying vegetables should also be cut into the same shape—cubes or squares, depending on the nature of the ingredient. However, when the dish calls for nuts such as cashews or peanuts, then the main ingredient has to be cut into the size of the nuts to match their natural shape.

The purpose of using a good amount of oil in cooking the poultry pieces is to enable the hot oil to float freely around each piece of meat and instantaneously seal the juices in. The oil keeps the pieces from sticking to each other or to the pan; it also assures each piece of meat the same temperature and provides heat from all sides throughout cooking. Hence, every piece is cooked uniformly. If you own a Teflon skillet, the meat can be cooked with less oil. Heat the skillet until hot, add enough oil to coat the pan; drop poultry pieces into hot oil, then toss and turn the pieces over with a spatula continuously until the meat is done. Immediately transfer the meat to a plate, then proceed with the other ingredients called for in the recipe.

A WORD ABOUT OIL

Any vegetable oil, such as corn oil, safflower oil, peanut oil, or cottonseed oil, is perfect for stir-frying. Good corn oil is preferred for deep-frying because it remains odorless when heated to a high temperature. Do not use olive oil; it is too rich and heavy. Butter should also be avoided because it burns easily and foods cooked with it do not taste authentically Chinese.

TO RECLAIM USED OIL FOR REUSE

After deep-frying, cool oil thoroughly. Pour the oil into a measuring cup or a jar through a fine wire strainer or a piece of cheesecloth. Store oil in the refrigerator. Reclaimed oil can be used just like fresh oil. Discard oil that has been used many times for deep-frying and has become brown in color.

STEAMING

There are two methods of steaming. In one, the food is placed in a shallow bowl or a Pyrex pie dish; the bowl or dish is then set in a pot which is filled with a few inches of water. The bowl or dish is supported by a rack, with the food uncovered but the pot tightly closed. The food is cooked by direct contact with the steam generated from the boiling water.

In the other method, the ingredients are put into a deep earthenware container covered with a lid, which is then placed either on a rack or directly inside a large pan filled with 2 inches of water. The large pan is then covered and the food in the container is cooked by the surrounding boiling water. The Yunnan Distilled Chicken Soup on page 263 is prepared in this way.

There are special utensils for steaming, some of bamboo and some of aluminum. The bamboo ones look like baskets; they come in several tiers, one set on top of the other and then covered with a bamboo lid that comes with the set. One of the disadvantages of bamboo steamers is they have to be set on top of a wok or some other large pan. If you only own one wok, the constant use of boiling water will damage the smooth coat of seasoning. Aluminum steamers are quite handy to have. A set usually comes with two tiers plus a bottom pot for water and a cover. The bottom of each tier is perforated to allow the easy flow of hot steam. You can also improvise with what is available in the kitchen by using a wok, a roasting pan, or a deep pot that has a lid, and a cake rack or a ring 2½ inches high made by removing both ends of a tin can. The rack is for supporting the plate of food to keep it away from the water. The edge of the plate should be about 1½ inches above the level of the water, so that when the water is boiling it will not splash into the plate. There also should be an inch of space between the plate and the edges of the pan to allow the steam to circulate. The water in the pot should be boiling vigorously at all times throughout the steaming period to generate enough steam to cook the food. During this time the pot should be covered tightly and should be uncovered as seldom as possible. For prolonged steaming, the boiling water must be replenished from time to time. After cooking is completed, turn off the heat, stand a little back from the pan before lifting up the cover, and allow the steam to disperse before removing the plate of food. To avoid burning your hands, wear a pair of rubber gloves while lifting the dish from the pan.

PREPARING CHICKEN STOCK

Chicken pieces such as necks, backs, carcasses, legs, or gizzards are perfect for making stock. An old hen or turkey necks and giblets also produce a very rich and flavorful stock. Chinese chicken stock is mild and quite subtle compared with a Western chicken or veal stock. Unlike a Western chicken broth, which often simmers with strong-flavored vegetables like onions, leeks, celery, carrots, and garlic, only rice wine, scallions, and ginger are added to the chicken or chicken pieces in making Chinese stock. Commercial canned chicken broth is a good substitute; however, it is heavily salted. When a large quantity of canned chicken broth is used, it should be diluted with water and the amount of salt in the recipe should be reduced. For every cup of canned chicken broth, add ½ cup water. When you are in a hurry and when only a small amount of stock is needed, bouillon cubes dissolved in water may be substituted.

To make Chinese chicken stocks you need:

> 3 lbs raw chicken carcasses, or necks, or legs, or
> gizzards and hearts, or trimmings
> 1 Tbsp Shao-sing wine, sake, or dry sherry
> 4 slices of fresh ginger, about 1 inch in diameter
> 2 large scallions with roots removed
> 8 cups water

Remove all fat and skin from chicken pieces. If chicken gizzards are used, remove yellow inside lining and the fat on the outside, rub gizzards with a couple of teaspoons of salt, rinse thoroughly with cold water, and drain.

Put chicken pieces in a large saucepan, add wine, ginger, scallions, and water; bring to a rapid boil over high heat. With a tablespoon skim off the foam that floats to the top; half a cup of cold water may be added to precipitate the scum. Cover pan and simmer over low heat for 3 hours. Strain stock through a fine strainer or a piece of cheesecloth. If stock is not to be used immediately, cool completely, put in containers, and freeze. Chicken broth can be frozen in any size containers for easy use in different recipes. Since chicken broth loses its flavor when refrozen, storing it in 1-cup or 1-pint containers will be more convenient. You can also freeze the chicken broth in ice cube trays and store the cubes in plastic bags.

PREPARING RICE

  ## BASIC BOILED RICE

1½   cups raw rice, long grain or short grain
3½   cups water

In a saucepan soak rice in 3½ cups of water for 30 minutes. (This is to give the rice a more fluffy texture; when you are in a hurry this step can be omitted.) Bring rice and water to a rapid boil over high heat and let boil for 3 minutes, stirring rice with a spoon once or twice. Cover saucepan tightly with a close-fitting lid; turn the heat down to low, and let it cook without lifting the cover for 20 minutes. Turn off heat and let rice sit tightly covered for 15 minutes. Before serving, loosen rice with a spoon. Makes about 5 cups. Serve 4.

INGREDIENTS

BAMBOO SHOOTS

In China there are many varieties of bamboo shoots and they grow at different times of the year. Some bamboo shoots are named after the four seasons, according to the time they are available. For instance, winter bamboo shoots are gathered at the end of winter before the young shoots become full grown. They are the tastiest of all bamboo shoots. Spring bamboo shoots are harvested in the spring; the shoots are very large, and most of the canned bamboo shoots are of this species. Canned bamboo shoots are obtainable in the United States. Once opened, they should be covered with water and stored in the refrigerator. Change the water three times a week and they will keep for a couple of months.

BEAN CURD, FERMENTED RED (NAN-RU)

Many cookbooks give the wrong definition for this ingredient. Because the Chinese name for this is "nan-ru," meaning "southern fermented bean curd," many people assume that it is *made* out of bean curd. However this special ingredient has nothing to do with soybeans or bean curd; instead it is made of taro root. Taro root is first steamed until tender, then mashed and blended with flour and salt and left in an earthen container for two weeks until it is covered with mold. It is then dried in the sun and formed into square pieces and covered with a mixture of rice wine, soy sauce, and saltpeter. After being aged for a couple of months it is ready for use. Very tasty when cooked with vegetables; it enhances their flavor.

BEAN CURD, FERMENTED WHITE (TOFU-RU)

Tofu-ru is somewhat like blue cheese, in that you either love it at first taste or you need a considerable length of time to appreciate its distinctive flavor. Though fermented bean curd does not have the same strong smell as blue cheese, its taste is equally sharp. The consistency of well-ripened tofu-ru is very soft and creamy; when put into the mouth it melts instantly.

Tofu-ru is fermented by leaving a firmer type of bean curd in a warm place (about 90°) for four to six days until the bean curd is covered with about ½ inch of mold. The fermented bean curd is then soaked in brine mixed with rice wine and spices. After aging for a couple of months, it is ready for use.

Tofu-ru sold in the United States usually comes in a jar; the pieces are about an inch square and are beige in color. There are plain and spiced varieties, and both will keep indefinitely in the refrigerator. Fermented bean curd can be added to all stir-fried vegetables; since it is quite salty, the amount of salt or soy sauce in the recipe should be reduced.

BEAN PASTE, SWEET

Sweet bean paste looks like ground brown bean paste (see below), but the color is dark brown instead of tan. Though it is called bean paste, it is made from flour and spices. Sweet bean paste comes packed in a small can; once open it should be transferred to a jar and stored in the refrigerator. Available in Oriental grocery stores. Hoisin sauce can be used as a substitute.

BEAN PASTE, SZECHUAN HOT BEAN OR SPICY SOY

Made the same way and contains the same ingredients as brown bean paste (see below), but with spicy chili added. It not only has all the subtle flavors of the brown bean sauce but has the extra zest of peppery chili. Hot bean paste comes in cans;

once opened, the paste should be transferred to a jar and kept in the refrigerator.

BEAN SPROUTS, MUNG

The sprouts of mung beans are milky white shoots with olive-green tops. They can be eaten raw, but the Chinese prefer to stir-fry them with meat and other vegetables or to blanch them in boiling water for a few seconds and serve them cold as salad. Available fresh in Chinese grocery stores or large supermarkets, they can also be grown at home. Mung bean sprouts are also available in cans but these are not a good substitute for fresh.

BOK CHOY

The most commonly used Chinese green vegetable. Bok choy somewhat resembles Swiss chard, only the stems are whiter and the leaves are darker. Sold fresh by the bunch in Chinese grocery stores or in the Oriental section of some supermarkets.

BROWN BEAN PASTE, OR
BROWN BEAN SAUCE

Made from soybeans and salt with flour added to serve as a fermenting agent. It is quite salty, but when a small amount is blended with vegetables or meat it enhances the flavor of the dish. Brown bean paste comes in two forms, one with the beans still whole, the other with beans ground up into a smooth paste. They are interchangeable as far as taste is concerned, except that the ground form blends in more evenly with delicate ingredients. Brown bean paste is sold in cans and in jars. Once the can is opened, the paste should be transferred to a jar and stored in the refrigerator. Available in Oriental grocery stores. Japanese soybean miso can be substituted.

CABBAGE CHINESE, OR NAPA CABBAGE, OR SAVOY CABBAGE

There are two varieties of this vegetable. One is thin and long, with stalks tightly packed together. The other is rounder, plumper, and slightly shorter. Both varieties can often be found in larger supermarkets, and they are interchangeable in all recipes. A whole head is usually too much to use for one meal, so seal the remaining part in a plastic bag, where it will keep for a couple of weeks when stored in the refrigerator.

CHEE-HOU SAUCE

Chee-hou is the name of a Cantonese from Fa-shan county who was famous for selling delicious braised and roast poultry. Because of the special sauce he conjured, people later on named the sauce after him. Chee-hou sauce is a combination of brown bean sauce, hoisin sauce, garlic, dried orange peel, rice wine, and sugar. Ready-made Chee-hou sauce is available in Oriental stores in Chinatown. It usually comes in a jar and will keep for a long time in the refrigerator.

CHILI PEPPER OIL (HOT OIL)

For those who love spicy food, chili oil is an indispensable condiment. Good chili oil is very hot, and only a couple drops are needed to perk up the taste of any dish. The variety made with sesame oil usually is not very strong. Available in Oriental markets; Tabasco sauce is an adequate substitute. See recipe on page 221 for homemade chili pepper oil.

CHILI PASTE, OR HOT PEPPER SAUCE

This paste of very hot red chili with added salt and rice wine can be used in cooking or can be served as a condiment. It comes in cans or jars; the Szechuan and Cantonese styles are interchangeable. Handle with care—one should start with small amounts and taste carefully before moving to larger quantities. Frequently this ingredient seems to increase in potency after the dish is cooked and set on the table.

CHILI PEPPERS, FRESH OR DRIED,
RED OR GREEN

Chili peppers come in many varieties, all of which are very hot. Usually the smaller ones are hotter, and when the seeds are left in, the strength is increased. Always remember not to rub your eyes while handling them. If dried ones are used, they should be soaked in hot water for half an hour before using. Canned Mexican red chilis can be substituted.

CHIVES, CHINESE

A member of the onion family, Chinese chives have a mild garlic flavor. A perennial, they are available from early summer until late August. The stems are ¼ inch wide, flat, and much darker in color than regular chives. They need a very short cooking time and are delicious as an herb in soups or when cooked with bean curd. The Chinese often stir-fry a large quantity and serve it as a vegetable. Chinese chives can be grown easily indoors or out. When stems reach a height of about 10 inches, cut them off and a new crop will start. Store chives in a sealed plastic bag; they will keep for one week in the refrigerator.

CLOUD EARS

See Tree Ears.

FERMENTED OR SALTED BLACK BEANS

A Cantonese specialty, fermented black beans are often used with garlic; both ingredients give a strong, distinctive flavor to dishes and should be used sparingly. Fermented black beans come in cans and plastic bags, and, once opened, should be transferred to a covered jar and stored in the refrigerator, where they will keep for months.

FERMENTED RED WINE LEES PASTE

Fermented red wine lees paste is a thick, burgundy-colored paste made by fermenting a mixture of glutinous rice, red rice, and wine yeast. After undergoing fermentation, the wine is strained out, and the sediment, which has a nutty wine taste, is used for flavoring pork and poultry. Federal law prohibits the importing of authentic fermented red wine lees paste into the States, but a locally made variety is available in some Oriental stores. See page 93 for a homemade version.

FIVE-SPICE POWDER

A reddish brown combination of five or sometimes six differ-ent ground spices including star anise, cloves, cinnamon, fen-nel, Szechuan peppercorns, and ginger. It is popularly used in Shanghai cooking to flavor meat dishes and pressed tofu, and sold in bottles or in plastic bags. It should be kept in a tightly sealed jar.

GINGER ROOT

An essential ingredient in Oriental cooking, ginger root grows in knotty, conjoined bulbs that look very much like iris rhizomes and has a pungent taste and refreshing aroma. It's used sliced, shredded, or minced. When buying ginger, select a plump chunk with smooth, shiny skin. Do not wash ginger; just scrape the skin off the portion that is needed and store the remaining part without wrapping in the vegetable compartment of the refrigerator, where it will keep for a couple of months. The skin may shrivel up but the taste will still be fresh. For full flavor, ginger should be sliced paper-thin or cut into fine slivers. When minced ginger is called for in a recipe, first cut the ginger into thin slices, then mash the pieces with the blunt side of the cleaver, and finally chop with the sharp edge. Ginger is quite easy to obtain nowadays and is available not only in Oriental grocery stores but often in supermarkets as well.

HOISIN SAUCE

A sweet reddish-brown sauce with a creamy consistency like catsup. It is a mixture of flour, soybeans, garlic, sugar, salt, and chili and can be used as a condiment or for cooking. Hoisin sauce is sold in cans or in jars; I prefer the canned variety. If transferred to a covered jar, it will keep for a long time in the refrigerator.

LICORICE ROOTS (GAM-CHO)

A perennial herb, about 2 to 3 feet high, licorice belongs to the pea family, grows in dry-climate areas, and is plentiful in Northern China and in North America from the Hudson Bay to North Mexico. The diameter of the root varies from ½ inch to 3 inches. The Chinese use the dried roots for cooking and medicinal purposes. They impart a sweet and cooling flavor. Many Chinese like to chew the roots to refresh their mouths. Cut-up licorice roots are available in Oriental grocery stores or Chinese medicine shops in Chinatown and will keep indefinitely. The roots look like thin dried branches, and when cut crosswise are bright yellow in the center. Licorice powder may be substituted for licorice roots.

LOTUS LEAVES

The beautiful umbrella-like leaves of the lotus plant come in various sizes. Large ones can be 2 feet in diameter. Both fresh and dried ones are used in many Cantonese dishes. They impart a delicate flavor and aroma to the food wrapped in them. Soak the leaves in hot water for a few hours and clean them with a sponge or a dish cloth before using them to wrap food. Dried lotus leaves are available in some Oriental grocery stores in Chinatown.

LOTUS SEEDS

The peanut-like seeds from the lotus pod come in cans or as dried nuts. The dried ones come either with a thin brown husk or blanched, and should be soaked before using. Because they symbolize fertility, they are quite often used in festival dishes.

MALTOSE SYRUP

This heavy, brownish syrup, made from buckwheat sugar, is thicker and less sweet than corn syrup or honey. It is used for glazing meat or for covering the skin of poultry to give it a crispy texture without burning when roasted or fried. A specialty of Kwangtung province, it usually comes in a small white or brown decorative crock. The consistency is thick, so it must be dug out with a strong spoon. Maltose syrup is available in Oriental grocery stores. White corn syrup can be used as a substitute.

MUSHROOMS, DRIED CHINESE OR DRIED BLACK

An elegant ingredient in Chinese cooking, they rank as high in prestige in Chinese cooking as do truffles in French dishes. There are many varieties of dried Chinese mushrooms; the most common ones available in the United States come from Japan. Dried mushrooms are rated by size; the larger and thicker the more costly. They should be stored in a cool and dry place or wrapped tightly and kept in the refrigerator. Before being used, they must be soaked in warm water for 15 minutes.

MUSHROOMS, STRAW OR GRASS

Only canned and dried straw mushrooms are sold in the United States. Canned ones have a crunchy texture and are used in stir-fried dishes. The dried ones are generally used in soups.

MUSTARD GREENS, CHINESE

A dark green vegetable with ruffled leaves and thick stems loosely wrapped into a head. It has a slightly bitter taste. Delicious in soups or cooked with fermented black beans and garlic. Available in some supermarkets; grows easily in any type of soil.

NOODLES, FRESH RICE

This kind of noodle is the favorite of the Cantonese; the name for it in Cantonese is *sa-haw-fun*. It is made by pouring a ¼-inch-thick layer of rice batter onto a large flat surface and steaming it until it becomes solid, then cutting the sheet into ½-inch-wide strips. Available in Chinese noodle shops and grocery stores, it also comes in dried form, but this is not a very satisfactory substitute for fresh.

NOODLES, MUNG BEAN, CELLOPHANE, VERMICELLI, BEAN THREAD, OR TRANSPARENT

Made from mung bean flour, these range in size from thin as a thread to thick as a string. They are packaged in 2- to 8-ounce skeins and are commonly used in stir-fried dishes, soups, and salads. Always sold dried, they become soft and translucent when cooked. Always soak mung bean noodles in hot water for 30 minutes before using.

OYSTER SAUCE

A rich thick sauce made of oysters, soy, and brine. It has a wonderful delicate flavor that gives zest to subtle or bland dishes. Store in the refrigerator after opening.

PARSLEY, CHINESE OR FRESH CORIANDER

An aromatic herb with a strong, distinctive flavor. Its leaves are serrated and resemble those of chervil. Available in Chinese grocery stores or in supermarkets that sell Spanish and Mexican ingredients. Usually comes with the root intact; should be stored in the refrigerator in a sealed plastic bag without rinsing or removing the roots. It is easy to grow fresh coriander at home; just plant ordinary coriander seeds either indoors or outdoors and they will grow very rapidly.

PLUM SAUCE, OR DUCK SAUCE

Plum sauce is a kind of sweet and sour Chinese chutney made from plums, apricots, ginger, vinegar, sugar, and spices. Generally used as a condiment for roast poultry or roast pork, it is available in cans or jars. If it comes in a tin can, transfer it to a jar and keep refrigerated. Plum sauce will keep for a very long time.

RADISHES, CHINESE, OR CHINESE TURNIPS

A Chinese radish resembles a giant icicle radish and is quite similar in taste. The Chinese name is *lo-bo;* the Japanese is *daikon.* Available in larger supermarket and Oriental grocery stores.

RED-IN-SNOW, OR PICKLED MUSTARD GREENS

This is a salty pickled vegetable made with what the West calls mustard greens. It is a bit bitter when cooked fresh, but the pickled variety has a divine taste. Red-in-snow adds a nice flavor to soups and to vegetables. It is available in large and small cans, but buy the small one if possible. If you transfer the unused portion to a covered jar, it will keep up to two months in the refrigerator.

RICE, GLUTINOUS OR SWEET

A short-grain rice of milky white color that becomes sticky when cooked. Used mostly for sweets.

SAUSAGE, CHINESE (LAAP-CHEUNG)

Chinese sausages are more slender than pepperoni; they are about ¾ inch in diameter and 6 inches long. Made of cut-up pork pieces cured in wine, soy sauce, sugar, and saltpeter, then stuffed in casings and dried, they are reddish in color and always tied in pairs, but sold by weight. If frozen, they can be kept for a long time and are very tasty when cooked whole with rice, then sliced into thin pieces, or cut up into ½-inch sections and browned in a skillet.

SESAME OIL

An aromatic oil made from roasted sesame seeds and light brown in color. The pale-colored variety sold in supermarkets is not processed the same way and cannot be used in recipes calling for sesame oil. Available in Oriental grocery stores.

SESAME PASTE

Made from ground toasted sesame seed, sesame paste comes in cans and jars and looks like unhomogenized peanut butter. Once opened, it should be kept in the refrigerator to prevent it from becoming rancid. Stir and blend evenly before each use to rehomogenize it. Peanut butter or tahini can be substituted for sesame paste, but neither has the same rich flavor. (Although tahini is also sesame paste, it is made from untoasted sesame seed and therefore lacks the nutty flavor and aroma.) Available in Oriental grocery stores.

SHAO-SING WINE, OR CHINESE RICE WINE

Light brown in color, this wine is made from rice and contains about 14 percent alcohol. It can be purchased from Chinese liquor stores and also from some regular liquor stores. Shao-sing wine can also be served as a drink when slightly heated. Japanese sake is an excellent substitute; when it is impossible to get either, use a dry sherry.

SHRIMP, DRIED

Dried shrimp are used as a seasoning agent to enhance vegetables, soups, and meat dishes. They have a very strong fish smell but impart a delicate flavor to subtle dishes. Most of the dried shrimp sold in the States are imported from Japan and Thailand, and range from ½ inch to 2 inches long. They are packed in plastic bags containing different amounts of shrimp and must be soaked in warm water before using. When stored in the freezer, they will last indefinitely.

SNOW PEAS

A special kind of pea that can be eaten whole—pod and all. They have a bright green color and are picked before the peas have matured. Available fresh or frozen in Oriental grocery stores and supermarkets.

SOUR MUSTARD GREENS

This is a Chinese sauerkraut, which is added to meat and fish to heighten the flavor or served alone as a side dish. The vegetable is soaked in brine until it starts to ferment and turns slightly sour. Mustard greens are dark green when fresh and have thick broad stems with ruffled leaves. Sour mustard greens become yellow after being soaked in brine for a while. They are available in Oriental grocery stores, sold in cans or jars, and should be stored in the refrigerator after being opened. See page 108 for a recipe for a homemade version.

SOY SAUCE

This most essential seasoning comes in many varieties, some quite dark in color and some light. In this cookbook the amount used in each recipe is based on an all-purpose soy sauce such as Tamari soy sauce, which is naturally fermented, or the Japanese brand, Kikkoman. Both types are readily available in most supermarkets and Oriental stores. Low-salt soy sauce is also available in health food stores.

SOY SAUCE, LIGHT OR THIN

Much lighter than Japanese all-purpose soy sauce, this is used mostly for more delicate and subtle dishes. If it is impossible to obtain light soy sauce, substitute Japanese all-purpose soy sauce.

STAR ANISE

This pretty herb looks like a star with eight corners and has a licorice-like flavor; it is related to the magnolia family. These star-shaped brown pods are the dried fruits of star anise trees; they grow mostly in Southeast China. Star anise is not related to Western-style anise, which is an herbal grass. It is sold dried in Oriental grocery stores, and will keep indefinitely if stored in a sealed container.

SZECHUAN PEPPERCORN

A reddish brown, mildly spicy aromatic pod that has a tiny black seed, about the same size as a regular peppercorn. Most Chinese grocery stores carry them. Store in a sealed container.

Szechuan Peppercorn Powder

3 Tbsps Szechuan peppercorns

Over a low flame, toast Szechuan peppercorns in an unoiled cast-iron skillet for about 5 minutes. Grind with mortar and pestle, then sift with a fine strainer. Save the powder which comes out of the strainer and discard the parts remaining in the strainer.

Szechuan Peppercorn Salt

3 Tbsps salt
2 Tbsps Szechuan peppercorns

Combine salt and Szechuan peppercorns in an unoiled cast-iron skillet and toast them over a low flame for about 5 minutes. Remove from fire and cool. Grind with mortar and pestle, then sift with a fine strainer. Use the powder which comes out of the strainer and discard the parts remaining in the strainer.

SZECHUAN PRESERVED VEGETABLE (JA-TSAI)

A salty, spicy pickle made from a kind of vegetable that grows in clusters of knobby stems. Sold in cans; once opened, it should be transferred to a clean covered jar and refrigerated. Will keep for months.

TANGERINE PEELS, DRIED

The longer these pieces of brownish dried tangerine peels have been kept, the better their flavor. Soak them in warm water before using. They add a subtle citrus flavor to braised poultry. Sold by weight and rather expensive, they can be made at home by hanging thin tangerine peels to dry in an airy place or a dry room, and will keep indefinitely.

TREE EARS, CLOUD EARS, OR WOOD EARS

A crunchy-textured fungus that grows on dead tree bark. When fresh it resembles human ears, hence the name tree ears or wood ears. Also called cloud ears because most of this kind of fungus comes from Yunnan Province (*yun* means cloud in Chinese). Sold by weight in Chinese grocery stores. Will keep indefinitely. Before using, soak tree ears in hot water for 30 minutes, then rinse thoroughly and cut off the woody part of the bottom.

TURNIPS, CHINESE

See *Radishes, Chinese.*

VINEGAR, CHINESE RED

This vinegar is made of rice and has a pale red color similar to that of rosé wine. It is not as strong and tangy as regular vinegar, and is known for its appealingly delicate taste. It can be bought in large- and small-size bottles and will keep indefinitely in the refrigerator. Use as a dip for noodles and seafood.

WATER CHESTNUTS

This ingredient is well known in the West. Water chestnuts are tubers of a plant that grows in marshes, and are dark brown in color with thin but tough skins. When peeled, the flesh is white, crisp, and sweet. Young water chestnuts are usually eaten raw as a fruit; more matured ones are used in cooked dishes. Peeling water chestnuts is very time-consuming; the canned ones, available at supermarkets, are perfectly good for cooking and save time.

CANTON AND
SOUTH CHINA

There is an old Chinese saying: "To be born in Soochow, to eat in Canton, to dress in Hangchow, and to die in Liouchow." Soochow is famous for its pretty girls, Canton for its excellent cuisine, Hangchow for its fine silk, and Liouchow for its good wood for making caskets. Perhaps not all Chinese will agree with the implication that Cantonese cooking is the best in the nation. Nevertheless, it has been a general conception for many generations. Certainly, the Cantonese people are famous for adding great numbers of exotic things to their menus. All creatures and plants are ingeniously incorporated into their cooking; be it snake, bear paw, rice sparrow, rice worm, frog, squab, or dog meat—all are dainties of the board.

Kwangtung Province is situated in southern China and has a subtropical climate where fruits, crops, and fresh vegetables grow all year round. Its long coastline and rivers offer fish and seafood of every variety, while the farms abound with chickens, ducks, geese, and squabs. Because they have had such a wide selection of natural ingredients and also comfortable living conditions, the Cantonese have been able to devote time to creating enormous varieties of delicacies to satisfy their interest in dining. Take Dim Sum, their teahouse snacks, for example. There are at least a hundred varieties of these delectable tidbits, and new dishes are still being introduced every season.

Since fresh ingredients are always available, the Cantonese are extremely mindful of preserving the natural flavor of food. Birds especially are prepared with rather simple cooking techniques. They are cooked with a minimum of heating and not a second longer than necessary. Poaching, steaming, open-fire roasting, and quick stir-frying are the most commonly used methods for cooking poultry. In order not to overpower the delicate taste of birds, great attention is also paid to flavoring them. In comparison with the cooking of other regions, Cantonese dishes are generally milder and more subtle. Salt and soy sauce are used sparingly and wisely. The appropriate color of soy sauce is added to a dish according to the nature of the ingredient. The flavor of dark soy sauce would be too dominating for a plain poached chicken; yet on the other hand, light soy sauce lacks the rich flavor and brown color needed for a bird poached in master sauce. In this chapter the Poached Chicken with Ginger and Scallion Sauce, Steamed Chicken with Mushrooms, Soy Sauce Squab, and Mu Goo Gai Pan are perfect testimony to the cooking techniques and careful seasoning of the school of Cantonese cookery.

Within this southern region there is one more popular cuisine which should be mentioned—the cooking of Chaochow. Chaochow is an area situated along the lower reaches of the Han River near the coast on the east border of Kwangtung Province. The distinguishing characteristic of Chaochow food lies in the art of skillful blending of good ingredients to accentuate their natural flavors. Great attention is also paid to the physical appearance of their food. In my opinion, they have the best goose dishes in the whole country. The poultry dishes are special not only for their scrumptious taste but also for their unique ingredients.

Another specialty from Chaochow is satay paste, a marvelous spicy concoction of ground peanuts, dried shrimp, dried flounder, sesame paste, garlic, shallots, chili pepper powder, five-spice powder, coriander seeds, mustard seeds, sugar, and salt, all pounded and blended together. The Stir-Fried Chicken with Satay Sauce and Braised Satay Chicken in this chapter are zesty, spicy, and incredibly delicious. Satay paste is widely available in Oriental stores. It comes in jars imported from Taiwan. The two brands sold in the United States are Lan Chi and Cow Head. Both companies, however, call their sauce barbecue sauce in English although the Chinese characters on the labels give the proper name, satay paste.

STIR-FRIED CHICKEN WITH ASPARAGUS

鸡
丁
炒
龙
须

- 8 oz boned chicken breast
- ½ Tbsp Shao-sing wine, sake, or dry sherry
- 1½ Tbsps soy sauce
- 1 Tbsp cornstarch
- 3 Tbsps oil
- ½ lb fresh asparagus
- 2 cups water
- 1 Tbsp brown bean paste
- ½ tsp sugar
- ½ Tbsp white or cider vinegar
- 1 tsp minced garlic
- 1 tsp minced ginger
- ½ tsp chili pepper oil (optional; see page 30)

Dice chicken and mix with wine, ½ Tbsp soy sauce, ½ Tbsp cornstarch, and 1 Tbsp oil.

Rinse asparagus; remove the tough part of each stalk, then cut the rest diagonally into ¾-inch pieces. In a saucepan, bring 2 cups water to a boil, drop in asparagus, and blanch for 3 to 4 minutes depending on the thickness of the stalks. Remove from water and drain. Reserve ½ cup of the water and cool.

In a small bowl combine brown bean paste with sugar, vinegar, the remaining 1 Tbsp soy sauce and ½ Tbsp cornstarch, and the asparagus stock.

Heat the remaining oil in a skillet or a wok over high heat; stir in garlic and ginger and cook for 10 seconds. Drop in chicken and stir continuously to separate the pieces. Cook until chicken becomes firm, about 1 minute. Add the mixture from the small bowl and the asparagus; stir until sauce is thickened. Blend in the chili pepper oil if desired. Serves 4.

炸子鸡 CANTONESE DEEP-FRIED CHICKEN

Poached in seasoned stock, glazed with a sweet and sour mixture, then fried till the skin is crisp, this fried chicken is wonderfully tender and juicy. It can be cut up into small pieces and served Chinese style or split in half and served with rice pilaf as a Western dinner for 2.

6 cups water
1 tsp salt
½ tsp Szechuan peppercorn
1 star anise
1 stick cinnamon
1 whole nutmeg, crushed
½ tsp fennel
3 slices of fresh ginger
3 scallions
1 chicken, about 3 lbs or less
3 Tbsps vinegar
1 Tbsp corn syrup
4 cups oil
1 Tbsp Szechuan peppercorn salt (see page 40)

In a saucepan bring 6 cups of water to a boil over moderate heat. Add salt, Szechuan peppercorn, anise, cinnamon stick, nutmeg, fennel, ginger, and scallions. Simmer all these ingredients in water for 15 minutes.

Wash chicken and drain. Poach the chicken in the spiced water for about 20 minutes. Drain and dry inside and out thoroughly with paper towels.

Mix vinegar and corn syrup together in a small bowl. Rub the chicken inside and out with the mixture. Tie the neck skin of the chicken with a piece of string and hang in an airy place, or by a window; or let an electric fan blow at the chicken for 5 hours. Let chicken air for 1 day or until the skin is dry.

In a wok or a deep-fryer heat 4 cups of oil until hot. Lower the chicken into the oil and fry over moderate heat for 10 to 15 minutes or until the chicken is crisp and golden brown.

Remove chicken from oil and drain. Following instructions on page 13, chop chicken into 1-inch by 2-inch pieces and arrange neatly on a platter. Serve at once with roasted Szechuan peppercorn salt. Serves 6.

CHICKEN EGG FU YUNG

鸡
丝
炒
芙
蓉
蛋

This recipe turns a few plain eggs into elegant party fare. Serve this dish as an appetizer in a multicourse Chinese or Western dinner.

- 6 oz boned chicken breast
- ½ Tbsp Shao-sing wine, sake, or dry sherry
- ¼ tsp salt
- ½ Tbsp cornstarch
- ½ egg white (optional)
- ¾ cup chicken stock, homemade (see page 23) or canned
- 2 Tbsps fresh or defrosted frozen peas
- ½ Tbsp soy sauce
  Dash white pepper
- ½ Tbsp cornstarch dissolved in 1 Tbsp water
- 1 tsp sesame oil
- ½ cup oil (see page 20 on stir-frying)
- 3 eggs, beaten
- ¼ cup sliced canned mushrooms
- ¼ cup finely shredded scallions

Following instructions on page 16, cut chicken into thin strips, then mix with wine, ⅛ tsp salt, and the cornstarch and egg white.

In a small saucepan bring stock, peas, and soy sauce to a boil, then add pepper. Thicken sauce with dissolved cornstarch and add sesame oil. Set aside and keep warm.

Heat oil in a wok over moderate heat until hot but not smoking, add chicken, stirring to separate the strips. Cook for about 40 seconds or until chicken meat turns white and firm; with a slotted spoon, scoop it into a bowl and cool for a few minutes. Add eggs, mushrooms, scallions, and the remaining ⅛ tsp salt. Transfer the remaining oil to a cup or a bowl and reserve.

Heat 1 Tbsp reserved oil in a skillet or a wok over moderate heat; pour in ⅓ of egg mixture. Swirl the pan to spread the mixture into a pancake about 4 inches in diameter. When the mixture is almost set, flip with a spatula and cook until egg becomes dry. Transfer to a serving plate and repeat with the rest of the egg mixture. Pour the hot sauce over the omelets and serve at once. Serves 4.

LEMON CHICKEN

柠
蒙
鸡

12 oz boneless chicken meat, white or dark
1 Tbsp Shao-sing wine, sake, or dry sherry
1½ Tbsps soy sauce
1 Tbsp cornstarch
1 small egg white
1 cup oil
1 tsp minced fresh ginger
½ cup chicken stock (see page 23)
2 Tbsps lemon juice
½ Tbsp sugar
¼ tsp salt
1 tsp cornstarch dissolved in 2 Tbsps water
½ Tbsp grated lemon rind
1 lemon, sliced

Remove chicken skin and cut meat into 1-inch by 2-inch pieces, about ¼ inch thick. Mix chicken with wine, 1 Tbsp soy sauce, and the cornstarch and egg white.

Heat the oil in a wok over moderate heat. When oil is hot but not smoking, drop in chicken. Stir and separate chicken in oil; cook for about 2 minutes. Remove chicken from oil with a slotted spoon and drain.

Empty all but 1 Tbsp of oil from wok. Set work back on moderate heat. Add ginger, then the stock, lemon juice, sugar, salt (omit salt if canned chicken stock is used), and the remaining ½ Tbsp soy sauce. Bring everything to a boil, then thicken the mixture with dissolved cornstarch. Add grated lemon rind and combine the cooked chicken with the sauce. Transfer chicken to a serving plate and decorate with sliced lemon. Serve at once. Serves 4.

POACHED CHICKEN WITH GINGER AND SCALLION SAUCE

葱油鸡

1   chicken (not frozen), 2½ to 3 lbs
2   quarts water
1   Tbsp Shao-sing wine, sake, or dry sherry
2   stalks of scallion
4   slices of ginger
1   Tbsp minced ginger
3   Tbsps finely chopped scallion
¼   tsp salt
4   Tbsps oil
1   Tbsp light soy sauce

Wash chicken thoroughly inside and out and drain.

Pour the water into a 3- or 4-quart pot, add wine, scallion stalks, and ginger slices. Bring liquid to a boil over high heat. Place chicken into pot and bring liquid to a rolling boil again. Cover pot and turn heat down to low; let chicken simmer gently for about 30 minutes. Turn chicken over once during simmering period. Remove pot from heat and let chicken soak in liquid for 1 hour. Discard the liquid.

Transfer chicken to a large bowl and cool thoroughly.

In a small heatproof bowl mix minced ginger and chopped scallion with salt. Heat oil in a small pan or in a wok until very hot and pour over ginger and scallions. Stir in light soy sauce.

Chop chicken into 1-inch by 2-inch pieces according to instructions on page 13, and arrange on a plate. Pour ginger and scallion sauce over chicken and serve. This dish can be prepared in advance and served at room temperature. Serves 6.

MOO GOO GAI PAN
(STIR-FRIED CHICKEN WITH MUSHROOMS)

蘇
菇
鸡
片

    1   whole chicken breast, about 1 lb, or 12 oz boned
          chicken breast
    ½   Tbsp Shao-sing wine, sake, or dry sherry
          Dash white pepper
    ½   tsp salt
    ½   Tbsp cornstarch
    1   small egg white
    1   cup fresh snow peas or 1 cup sliced celery
    ½   lb fresh mushrooms
    1   cup oil (see page 20 on stir-frying)
    1   tsp minced ginger
    1   tsp minced garlic
    ¼   tsp sugar
    1   Tbsp oyster sauce
    1   tsp cornstarch dissolved in 1 Tbsp water

Skin and bone chicken breast according to instructions on page 15. With a sharp knife, slice chicken into very thin slices, about 1 inch by 1½ inches. In a bowl mix chicken with wine, white pepper, ¼ tsp salt, and the cornstarch and egg white; set aside.

Snap off both ends of each snow pea and remove the tough string on the sides. Rinse snow peas with cold water and drain.

Rinse fresh mushrooms in cold water, then pat dry with paper towels. Cut mushrooms into ¼-inch slices.

Heat oil in a wok or skillet over moderate heat. When oil is hot, add sliced chicken. Stir and separate chicken in oil until the meat turns white. Remove chicken from oil and drain.

Empty all but 1 Tbsp oil from the pan and reserve. Set pan and oil over high heat. Add snow peas and stir-fry for 30 seconds. Remove snow peas to a plate.

Set the wok or skillet on top of the heat, add 2 Tbsps reserved oil, drop in mushrooms, add the remaining ¼ tsp salt, and stir and cook for 1 minute. Transfer mushrooms to the same plate with the snow peas and set aside. Add 1 Tbsp oil to the pan and then drop in ginger and garlic; cook for a few seconds. Add chicken, sugar and oyster sauce, then combine the vegetables with the chicken. Stir and mix all the ingredients thoroughly. Stir in the dissolved cornstarch; cook until the sauce becomes thick. Transfer everything to a platter and serve at once. Serves 4.

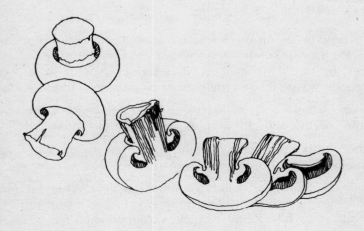

CHICKEN WITH CASHEWS

腰果鸡丁

> 12 oz boned chicken breast
> 1 Tbsp Shao-sing wine, sake, or dry sherry
> ¼ tsp salt
> 4 tsps cornstarch
> 1 small egg white
> 1 Tbsp oyster sauce or soy sauce
> ½ tsp sugar
> 1 tsp sesame oil
> 2 Tbsps water
> 1 cup oil (see page 20 on stir-frying)
> 1 cup raw cashews
> 4 slices of ginger, about 1 inch in diameter
> 3 scallions, cut into 1-inch sections

Dice chicken into ½-inch cubes according to instructions on page 17. Mix with ½ Tbsp wine, the salt, 3 tsps cornstarch, and the egg white.

In a small bowl combine oyster sauce, sugar, sesame oil, 2 Tbsps water, and the remaining ½ Tbsp wine and 1 tsp cornstarch.

Heat oil in a wok over moderate heat until hot but not smoking; drop in cashews and fry until they become light brown. Remove nuts from oil with a slotted spoon and drain. Add chicken to oil, stirring to separate the pieces; cook until meat becomes firm, about 1 minute. Remove chicken from oil and drain. Empty all but 1 Tbsp oil from wok, set over high heat; add ginger and scallions. Stir and cook for 20 seconds; add chicken and the sauce from the bowl. Coat chicken with the sauce evenly. When sauce becomes thick, blend in the cashew nuts. Transfer to a plate and serve at once. Serves 4.

鸡条酸梅 FRIED CHICKEN STRIPS WITH PLUM SAUCE

    1   lb boned chicken, either white or dark meat
    1   Tbsp Shao-sing wine, sake, or dry sherry
    ⅛   tsp salt
    1½ Tbsps soy sauce
    ⅔   cup flour
    ⅓   cup cornstarch
    ⅔   cup water
    2   cups oil
    ½   Tbsp minced garlic
    ⅓   cup canned plum sauce
    ½   Tbsp sugar
    ⅔   cup water or pineapple juice
    ½   Tbsp cornstarch dissolved in 1 Tbsp water

Cut chicken in strips 2 inches long by ½ inch wide by ½ inch thick. Mix chicken with wine, salt, and 1 Tbsp soy sauce. Set aside.

In a bowl mix flour and cornstarch with water until smooth, then blend in 1 Tbsp oil.

Heat 1 Tbsp oil in a small saucepan, stir in garlic, and cook for 15 seconds. Add plum sauce, sugar, water or pineapple juice, and the remaining ½ Tbsp soy sauce. Bring to a boil, then thicken with dissolved cornstarch. Keep warm.

Heat the remaining oil in a wok or deep-fryer over moderate heat until 350°. Dip chicken strips into the batter and deep-fry 10 to 12 pieces at a time until golden brown, about 3 minutes. Remove from oil and drain. Repeat with the rest of the chicken. Place chicken on a plate, then pour hot plum sauce over it and serve at once. Serves 4.

BRAISED CHICKEN WITH TIGER LILY BUDS

南
乳
焗
鸡

The botanical name for tiger lily is Yellow Day-Lily or Lemon Lily. A native of eastern Asia, these flowers grow wild in China's northern region. The dried buds sold in Oriental grocery stores look like little brown twigs and are about 3 inches long. They are used extensively in Chinese vegetarian cooking.

    40 tiger lily buds
     2 lbs chicken with bones, 1 whole breast and 2 legs,
            or all legs
     2 Tbsps soy sauce
     2 Tbsps oil
     1 Tbsp minced garlic
     2 Tbsps mashed fermented red bean curd
     2 Tbsps Shao-sing wine, sake, or dry sherry
    ½ Tbsp minced ginger
    ¾ cup chicken stock (see page 23)
     1 tsp sugar
    ½ Tbsp cornstarch dissolved in 1 Tbsp water
     1 tsp sesame oil

Place tiger lily buds in a bowl and cover with hot water. Soak for 15 minutes, then rinse with clear water. Cut off tough stem ends, then cut each bud in half crosswise.

Split the chicken breast lengthwise into two, then cut each piece crosswise into 1½-inch pieces. Separate the chicken thighs and drumsticks. Cut the thighs crosswise into two equal pieces; cut each drumstick crosswise in two. Mix chicken with soy sauce.

Heat oil in a wok or a saucepan over moderate heat; stir in garlic and fermented red bean curd. Cook for 15 seconds in hot oil. Drop in chicken; coat the chicken pieces with the garlic and fermented bean curd paste. Add wine, ginger, tiger lily buds, and stock. Cover and simmer over low heat for 20 minutes.

Uncover, add sugar, then thicken sauce with dissolved cornstarch. Stir in sesame oil and transfer to a plate and serve. This dish can be prepared in advance and reheated. Serves 4 to 6.

豉油鸡 SOY SAUCE CHICKEN CANTONESE STYLE

        1   chicken (never frozen), about 3 lbs
        1   tsp Szechuan peppercorns
        2   whole star anise
        6   cloves
        4   slices of licorice roots or 1 tsp licorice powder
        1   tsp fennel seeds
     1½   cups soy sauce
        2   nutmegs, slightly crushed
        1   cinnamon stick
        ½   cup Shao-sing wine or sake (no other substitute)
        2   cups water or chicken stock (see page 23)
        4   slices of fresh ginger
        ½   cup rock candy or 2 Tbsps sugar

Wash chicken thoroughly and remove the yellow layer of tissue from skin. Dry chicken and let it air for 15 minutes.

Tie peppercorns, anise, cloves, licorice, and fennel seeds in cheesecloth.

In a heavy 3- to 4-quart pan, combine soy sauce, nutmegs, cinnamon stick, wine, water or stock, ginger, rock candy, and the bag of spices and herbs. Bring stock to a boil over high heat. Then cover pan and turn the heat down to low and simmer for 20 minutes. (This sauce can be prepared ahead of time and kept in refrigerator or freezer.)

Put chicken into the stock and bring to a boil. Cover pan and simmer chicken over low heat for 30 minutes. Turn chicken over a couple of times during simmering period. Remove pan from heat and leave chicken in stock for 1 hour. Transfer chicken to plate and cool.

Chop chicken into 1-inch by 2-inch pieces according to instructions on page 13, on how to carve cooked poultry Chinese fashion. Arrange neatly on a plate, and serve. Serves 6.

咖哩鸡腿 BRAISED DRUMSTICKS IN CURRY SAUCE

3 Tbsps oil
8 chicken drumsticks
½ Tbsp minced ginger
½ cup chopped scallions
1 Tbsp Indian curry paste or curry powder, more or
     less according to your taste
1 cup diced tomato
¼ tsp salt
2 Tbsps soy sauce
½ tsp sugar
¼ cup water
½ Tbsp cornstarch dissolved in 1 Tbsp water

Heat oil in a heavy pan over moderate heat; fry drumsticks until they become slightly brown. Remove drumsticks from pan. Add ginger and scallions. Stir in hot oil for 20 seconds, then mix in the curry paste or powder. Add tomato, salt, soy sauce, sugar, water, and the browned chicken drumsticks. Coat the drumsticks with the sauce, then cover and simmer over a low heat for 30 minutes. Uncover; thicken sauce with dissolved cornstarch. Arrange the drumsticks on a platter and pour sauce over them. This dish can be prepared in advance and reheated. Serves 4.

豉 椒 鸡 丁 CHICKEN WITH PEPPER IN BLACK BEAN SAUCE

12 oz boned chicken, either white or dark meat
1 Tbsp Shao-sing wine, sake, or dry sherry
½ Tbsp soy sauce
2 tsps cornstarch
1 large green pepper
2 Tbsps fermented black beans
½ Tbsp minced garlic
½ cup oil (see page 20 on stir-frying)
2 cups diced fresh mushrooms (optional)
½ Tbsp chopped fresh chili pepper or 1 tsp chili
    pepper oil (optional; see page 30)
1 Tbsp oyster sauce
¼ tsp sugar

Dice chicken into ½-inch cubes according to instructions on page 17. In a bowl mix chicken with wine, soy sauce, and cornstarch.

Cut pepper in half; remove and discard seeds; rinse. Cut into 1-inch squares.

Rinse black beans and mash them with mortar and pestle, or put the beans in a small bowl and pound them with the handle of a cleaver. Mix in garlic.

Heat 1 Tbsp oil in a wok or a skillet over moderate heat; add pepper and stir-fry for about 1 minute. Remove pepper to a plate. If mushrooms are used, cook them the same way for 2 minutes and transfer to the same plate with the pepper.

Heat the remaining oil in a wok or a skillet over moderate heat until hot but not smoking. Drop in chicken, stir to separate the pieces, and cook until meat becomes firm, about 1 minute. With a slotted spoon, remove chicken from oil and drain. Empty all but 1 Tbsp oil from wok; add the black beans and garlic. If chopped chili pepper is used, drop it in too. Stir everything in hot oil for 10 seconds. Return cooked chicken to pan, add oyster sauce and sugar, and mix well. Blend in pepper and mushrooms (if used). Transfer the mixture to a plate and serve. Serves 4.

蚝油手撕鸡 CHICKEN STRIPS WITH OYSTER SAUCE

6 *Chinese black mushrooms, about 1½ inches in diameter*
½ *cup water*
1 *cup fresh bean sprouts or ½ cup shredded bamboo shoots*
1 *lb boned chicken breast*
1 *Tbsp Shao-sing wine, sake, or dry sherry*
¼ *tsp salt*
  Dash white pepper
1 *Tbsp cornstarch*
1 *egg white*
2 *Tbsps oyster sauce*
¼ *tsp sugar*
1 *tsp sesame oil*
½ *Tbsp cornstarch dissolved in 2 Tbsps stock*
1 *cup oil (see page 20 on stir-frying)*
1 *Tbsp finely shredded fresh ginger*
1 *tsp minced garlic*

Soak mushrooms in hot water for 15 minutes and reserve the water. Remove stems from mushrooms and cut the caps into fine slivers. Put mushrooms in a small saucepan and add the reserved water. Cover and simmer for 15 minutes over low heat.

Rinse bean sprouts in cold water and drain. Set aside.

Cut chicken into thin strips about 2 inches long, according to instructions on page 16. In a bowl mix chicken strips with wine, salt, pepper, cornstarch, and egg white.

In a small bowl combine oyster sauce, sugar, sesame oil, and the dissolved cornstarch.

Heat oil in a wok over moderate heat. When oil is hot, add chicken. Separate chicken strips while cooking. Cook until meat becomes firm and white, about 1 minute. With a strainer, remove chicken from oil and drain.

Empty all but 1 Tbsp oil from wok and reserve the rest. Set wok over a high heat, drop in bean sprouts, and stir-fry for 10 seconds. Remove to a plate.

Add 1 Tbsp reserved oil to the wok; drop in ginger and garlic. Then add chicken, mushrooms, bean sprouts, and the sauce. Stir and cook until sauce is thickened. Transfer everything to a serving platter and serve at once. Serves 4.

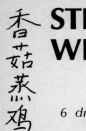

STEAMED CHICKEN WITH MUSHROOMS

     6 dried Chinese black mushrooms, about 1½ inches
          in diameter
    12 oz chicken meat or 1½ lb chicken with bones
     1 Tbsp Shao-sing wine, sake, or dry sherry
    ⅛ tsp salt
    ½ Tbsp soy sauce
    ¼ tsp sugar
    ½ Tbsp cornstarch
     4 slices of ginger, about 1 inch in diameter
     1 Tbsp oil

Rinse mushrooms in cold water, then cover them with ½ cup warm water and let stand for 30 minutes. Remove and discard stems. Cut the caps into halves.

Cut chicken into 1-inch squares. (If the chicken has bones, chop into 1½-inch pieces.) Mix chicken with wine, salt, soy sauce, sugar, and cornstarch. Put the chicken in a shallow bowl or a pie dish; blend in mushrooms and ginger. Sprinkle with oil. Steam chicken for 15 minutes according to the instructions on page 21. Serve at once. Serves 4.

DICED CHICKEN WITH ALMONDS

杏
仁
鸡
丁

  12 oz boned chicken breast
   1 Tbsp Shao-sing wine, sake, or dry sherry
  ¼ tsp salt
1½ Tbsps cornstarch
   1 small egg white
   1 Tbsp soy sauce
  ½ tsp sugar
      Dash white pepper
   1 Tbsp oyster sauce
   3 Tbsps chicken stock or water (see page 23)
  ½ tsp sesame oil
   1 cup oil (see page 20 on stir-frying)
  ½ cup blanched whole almonds
   1 cup diced green pepper
  ½ cup diced canned straw mushrooms or button
      mushrooms
   3 Tbsps chopped scallion
   1 tsp minced ginger

Dice chicken breast according to instructions on page 17. In a bowl mix chicken with wine, salt, 1 Tbsp cornstarch, and the egg white.

In a small bowl combine soy sauce, sugar, pepper, oyster sauce, stock, sesame oil, and the remaining ½ Tbsp cornstarch.

Heat oil in a wok or a skillet over moderate heat until hot but not smoking. Drop in almonds and deep-fry until the nuts turn light brown. Remove from oil and drain. Add chicken to the oil, stir to separate the pieces, and cook until firm and white. With a slotted spoon, remove chicken from oil and drain. Empty all but 1½ Tbsps oil from the pan and heat over high heat; add green pepper, mushrooms, scallion, and ginger. Stir-fry for 1 minute, then add chicken and the mixture from the small bowl, blend thoroughly, and cook until sauce is thickened. Add almonds. Transfer to a plate and serve. Serves 4.

BRAISED CHICKEN WINGS WITH OYSTER SAUCE

蚝
油
鸡
翼

10 chicken wings
 2 Tbsps oil
 4 slices of ginger, about 1 inch in diameter
 3 scallions, cut into 3-inch sections
 1 Tbsp Shao-sing wine, sake, or dry sherry
1½ Tbsps soy sauce
1½ Tbsps oyster sauce
 1 tsp sugar
 ½ cup chicken stock (see page 23) or water

Rinse chicken wings and dry with paper towels. Chop off and discard the tip of each chicken wing; cut the remaining section apart at the joint.

Heat oil in a wok or a saucepan over moderate heat. Drop in ginger and scallions and stir and cook for 20 seconds. Add chicken wings and brown and turn the pieces around with a spatula for 1 minute. Add the rest of the ingredients, cover, and cook for 20 minutes. Uncover, discard ginger and scallions, turn up heat, and boil until most of the liquid has evaporated. Transfer to a plate and serve hot or cold. Serves 4.

VELVET CHICKEN CORN SOUP

This light and fluffy soup is for formal dining, one of the favorites on banquet tables. To give extra flavor to the soup, use rich chicken stock as a base.

- 6 oz boned chicken breast
- 3½ cups chicken stock
- ½ Tbsp Shao-sing wine, sake, or dry sherry
- 1 8-oz can of creamed corn
- 1 large egg white
- ½ tsp salt
- 2 Tbsps cornstarch dissolved in ¼ cup water
- Dash white pepper
- 1 Tbsp minced cooked Smithfield ham

Puree chicken according to instructions on page 17. Mix chicken with wine and ½ cup creamed corn.

Beat egg white until frothy and fold into the chicken mixture.

In a big saucepan bring the remaining chicken stock to a boil, add salt and the remaining creamed corn. Bring soup to a boil, then thicken with dissolved cornstarch. When soup becomes thick, stir in the chicken mixture. As soon as the soup boils again, remove from heat, add pepper, pour into a tureen, sprinkle chopped ham on top, and serve at once. Serves 6.

Note: 4 oz cooked crab meat may be added to the soup just before adding the chicken mixture.

CHICKEN GIZZARDS AND WATERCRESS EGG DROP SOUP

西
洋
菜
鸡
腎
汤

This is a very easy, economical, and tasty soup. Chicken gizzards and watercress provide it with a delicate, subtle flavor.

- ½ lb chicken gizzards
- 4 cups water
- 2 cups coarsely chopped watercress
- 1 tsp salt
- 2 eggs, beaten
- Dash black pepper

Remove fat from gizzards; check the inside of each one and peel off the yellow lining if any. Rinse thoroughly, then cut gizzards into thin slices.

In a saucepan cover gizzards with the water; bring to a rolling boil. Cover and simmer over low heat for 1 hour or until gizzards are tender. Add watercress and salt; simmer uncovered for 5 minutes. Turn off heat and slowly stir in the eggs. When eggs are set, pour into a tureen, and sprinkle pepper over soup. Serves 6.

SWEET AND SOUR CHICKEN LIVERS

烧
焗
凤
肝

1 lb chicken livers
½ Tbsp Shao-sing wine, sake, or dry sherry
1 Tbsp cornstarch
3 Tbsps catsup
1 Tbsp Worcestershire sauce
½ Tbsp sugar
1 Tbsp soy sauce
2 Tbsps water
1 cup oil
1 tsp minced ginger

Rinse chicken livers and drain until very dry. Separate each pair in two, then cut each half crosswise into ¾-inch pieces. Marinate livers with wine and cornstarch for 15 minutes.

In a small bowl combine catsup, Worcestershire sauce, sugar, soy sauce, and water.

Heat oil in a wok over high heat; when oil is hot add livers and fry until brown and slightly dry, about 3 minutes. (Caution: Protect your arms from oil splatter by wearing long sleeves and standing a couple of feet away from the pan.) Remove liver with a slotted spoon and drain. Empty all but 1 Tbsp oil from wok; add ginger and catsup mixture to wok, then bring to a boil. Add liver and cook and stir for 30 seconds. Transfer to a plate and serve hot or cold. Serves 4.

CANTONESE ROAST DUCK

广
东
烧
鸭'

1 duck, about 5 lbs
1 Tbsp oil
3 cloves garlic, crushed
3 Tbsps Chee-hou sauce or 2 Tbsps ground bean
    sauce mixed with 1 Tbsp hoisin sauce
4 sections of a star anise, crushed
½ tsp Szechuan peppercorns, crushed
1 small cinnamon stick
½ cup water
1 scallion, cut into 3 or 4 sections
2 Tbsps Shao-sing wine or sake
¼ tsp salt
2 Tbsps malt syrup, corn syrup, or honey
3 Tbsps white vinegar
  Trussing needle and string

Rinse duck well with hot water. Dry the cavity and outside of duck with paper towels.

Heat oil in a saucepan, add crushed garlic. Cook for a few seconds, then add Chee-hou sauce, anise, peppercorns, cinnamon stick, water, scallion, 1 Tbsp wine, and the salt. Simmer all these ingredients over a low flame for 3 minutes. Remove sauce from fire and cool to lukewarm.

In a small bowl mix malt syrup with vinegar and the remaining 1 Tbsp wine.

Truss the opening of duck neck closely and tightly. Stand the duck upright on its neck and pour the cooked mixture into the cavity. Truss the tail opening securely, making sure that no liquid can run out. Brush duck skin thoroughly with the syrup mixture, reserving any that remains.

Place duck on a rack over a roasting pan. Roast in a 400° oven for 30 minutes, then reduce the temperature to 350° and roast for 30 minutes. Again reduce temperature to 300° and roast for another 30 minutes. Baste with syrup mixture every 20 minutes during roasting period.

Remove duck from oven and cool for 30 minutes. Remove trussing strings from tail opening and drain the sauce from the cavity into a bowl.

Chop duck into 1-inch by 2-inch pieces according to instructions on page 13, and arrange neatly on a platter. Strain the sauce and pour it over the duck evenly. Serves 6.

SWEET AND SOUR DUCK WITH PINEAPPLE

菠萝鸭块

- 12 oz boned duck breast
- 1 Tbsp Shao-sing wine, sake, or dry sherry
- ¼ tsp salt
- 1½ Tbsps cornstarch
- 1 small egg white
- ½ cup pineapple juice or chicken stock
- 1 Tbsp vinegar
- ½ Tbsp sugar
- 1 tsp sesame oil
- 1 cup oil (see page 20 on stir-frying)
- ½ Tbsp minced ginger
- 1 tsp minced garlic
- 1 Tbsp chopped fresh or pickled chili pepper
- 2 Tbsps chopped scallion
- 6 slices canned pineapple, cut into 2-inch sections

Slice duck meat into thin 1-inch by 2-inch pieces, according to instructions on page 16. Mix with ½ Tbsp wine, the salt, 1 Tbsp cornstarch, and the egg white.

In a small bowl combine pineapple juice or stock with vinegar, sugar, sesame oil, and the remaining ½ Tbsp cornstarch and ½ Tbsp wine.

Heat oil in a wok over moderate heat until hot but not smoking. Drop in duck, stir to separate the pieces, and cook until meat becomes firm, about one minute. With a slotted spoon, remove duck from oil and drain. Empty all but 2 Tbsps oil from wok, set over high heat, and add ginger, garlic, pepper, and scallion. Stir mixture in oil for 30 seconds, add cooked duck, then add the sauce mixture. Cook until sauce is thickened. Blend in pineapple. Transfer to a platter and serve. Serves 4.

STIR-FRIED TURKEY WITH OYSTER SAUCE

蚝
油
火
鸡

- 10 oz boned turkey breast
- ½ Tbsp Shao-sing wine, sake, or dry sherry
- ¼ tsp salt
  Dash white pepper
- 1 Tbsp cornstarch
- 1 small egg white
- 2 medium-sized green peppers
- ½ cup oil (see page 20 on stir-frying)
- ½ Tbsp minced garlic
- 1½ Tbsps oyster sauce
- ¼ tsp sugar

Dice turkey into ½-inch cubes; mix with wine, ⅛ tsp salt, and the white pepper, cornstarch, and egg white.

Cut green peppers in halves, remove and discard seeds. Cut into ¾-inch squares.

Heat oil in a wok or skillet until hot but not smoking; drop in turkey and stir to separate the pieces; cook for 2 minutes. With a slotted spoon, remove turkey from oil and drain. Empty all but 1 Tbsp oil from pan and reserve the rest; add green pepper and the remaining ⅛ tsp salt. Stir-fry green peppers for 1 minute; transfer to a plate.

Add 1 Tbsp reserved oil to the pan, stir in garlic, and cook for 15 seconds; add turkey, oyster sauce, sugar, and green peppers. Transfer to a serving plate. Serves 4.

STIR-FRIED TURKEY OR CHICKEN WITH SATAY SAUCE

10   oz boned turkey or chicken breast
½   Tbsp Shao-sing wine, sake, or dry sherry
¼   tsp salt
1   Tbsp cornstarch
1   small egg white
2   medium-sized green peppers
1   cup oil (see page 20 on stir-frying)
1   Tbsp soy sauce
½   tsp sugar
1½   Tbsps satay sauce
½   cup coconut milk (optional)
1   tsp cornstarch dissolved in 1 Tbsp water (omit
        dissolved cornstarch if coconut milk is not used)

Cut turkey or chicken into thin strips about 2 inches long according to instructions on page 16. Mix meat with wine, salt, cornstarch, and egg white.

Rinse green peppers and dry. Cut lengthwise in two; remove stems and seeds. Cut peppers into thin strips.

Heat oil in a wok over moderate heat until hot but not smoking, add turkey or chicken. Stir and separate meat in oil, cook for 2 minutes. With a slotted spoon remove turkey or chicken from oil and drain.

Empty all but 1 Tbsp oil from wok. Drop in green peppers and stir-fry over high heat for 1 minute. Push green peppers to the sides of the wok. Return cooked turkey or chicken to the center of the wok; add soy sauce, sugar, satay sauce, and coconut milk; blend everything thoroughly. Stir in dissolved cornstarch and then mix green peppers with turkey or chicken mixture. Transfer to a plate and serve at once. Serves 4.

汕头卤鹅 SWATOW COLD SOY SAUCE GOOSE OR DUCK

Swatow is a seaport situated on the east coast of Kwangtung Province. The people there speak a language that is related to the Amoy dialect of Fukien Province. The food from Swatow is called Chaochow cooking; it is famous all over southeastern China, Thailand, Singapore, and Malaysia.

Master sauce (see page 18) is the basis of many Cantonese poultry dishes—from chicken, duck, goose, and pigeon to sparrow. Swatow Cold Soy Sauce Goose or Duck is richer in flavor than other soy sauce poultry dishes of Canton. When poaching Swatow goose or duck with the master sauce, add only half of the amount of water listed. This is an extremely tasty dish and since it is always served cold, you can prepare it a couple of days in advance. Makes a great appetizer course.

- 1 goose, about 8 pounds (or 1 duck, about 5 pounds)
- 4 Tbsps salt (3 Tbsps for duck)
- 3 cups soy sauce (2 cups for duck)
- 1 cup Shao-sing wine, sake, or dry sherry (⅔ cup for duck)
- 8 slices of fresh ginger (6 slices for duck)
- 2 tsps Szechuan peppercorns (1 tsp for duck)
- 2 tsps fennel seeds (1 tsp for duck)
- 5 whole star anise (3 for duck)
- 16 cloves (12 for duck)
- 2 cinnamon sticks (1 for duck)
- 4 nutmegs (3 for duck)
- 12 slices of licorice root about ½ inch in diameter (9 slices for duck)
- 4 cups water (3 cups for duck)

Rinse and dry the goose or duck thoroughly with paper towels. Remove and discard large pieces of fat. Rub the bird inside and out with salt and let stand for ½ hour. Choose a pot that will fit the goose or the duck snugly and accommodate the sauce, the spices, and the water. (An oval enamel roasting pan is perfect for a goose or a duck.) Add the rest of the ingredients, except the water, to the pot and bring to a boil. Cover and simmer over low heat for 20 minutes.

Uncover the pot, place the bird in the sauce, and raise the heat to high. Boil the bird for 10 minutes; turn and coat the entire bird with the sauce. Add water, cover and simmer over moderate heat, 1½ hours for a goose, 1 hour for a duck. Turn the bird a few times for even cooking. Remove from stock and brush the skin with sesame oil. Set the goose in a colander with the tail opening facing down, or hang the bird up. Drain and cool for at least 4 hours. Carve according to instructions on page 13 and arrange neatly on a platter. Serve cold. Serves 8 to 10.

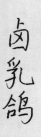

SOY SAUCE PIGEON OR CORNISH HEN

2 pigeons, or Cornish Hens, about 1 lb each
  Master sauce (see page 18), enough to cover the
    birds
1 tsp sesame oil

Wipe pigeons with a piece of damp cloth or paper towels. Poach pigeons in master sauce for 30 minutes over moderate heat. Remove them from the sauce and drain in a colander with the tail ends facing down. Brush the skin with sesame oil and let cool to lukewarm or room temperature. Following instructions on page 13 on how to carve cooked poultry, cut up the pigeons into bite-sized pieces, and place on a serving platter. Serves 4 to 6.

SOY SAUCE RICE SPARROWS

卤
禾
花
雀

Rice sparrows are a specialty along the Pear River Delta. The Cantonese consider them delicacies and prize them highly. When in season, rice sparrows are served at elegant dinners to honored guests. In the autumn during harvest time, flocks of them land on the rice fields to feed. The farmers take revenge by catching them and selling them to restaurants. Any small birds of the sparrow type, wild or domestic, can be substituted for rice sparrows.

12 rice sparrows, cleaned
 2 Tbsps Shao-sing wine, sake, or dry sherry
 2 Tbsps soy sauce
 ½ Tbsp salt
 1 tsp sugar
 ½ Tbsp minced ginger
 1 Tbsp oil
 1 Tbsp minced garlic
   Master sauce (see page 18), enough to cover the
     sparrows

Wipe sparrows with a damp cloth or paper towels. Mix wine, soy sauce, salt, sugar, and ginger, then rub the mixture all over the sparrows. Let stand for 30 minutes.

Heat oil in a saucepan, stir in garlic, and cook for 10 seconds. Add master sauce and bring to a boil. Poach sparrows in the master sauce for 10 minutes. Remove sparrows from the sauce and drain. Serve them whole at room temperature. Serves 4.

柱侯子鸡 CORNISH GAME HEN IN HOISIN SAUCE AND BROWN BEAN SAUCE

A remarkable bird, Cornish game hen certainly isn't a fowl that is used in traditional Chinese fare. However, this meaty bird blends perfectly with soy sauce and can be transformed into a deceptively Chinese dish. Moreover, Cornish game hen is readily available and more economical than pigeons, which the Chinese prepare in a similar manner.

> 2 small Cornish game hens
> 1 Tbsp minced garlic
> 1 Tbsp hoisin sauce
> 2 Tbsps brown bean paste, mashed
> 2 Tbsps oil
> 1 small piece of dried orange peel, about 1 inch by 2 inches
> 1 Tbsp Shao-sing wine, sake, or dry sherry
> 1 Tbsp soy sauce
> ½ tsp salt
> ½ tsp sugar
> ½ Tbsp cornstarch dissolved in 1 Tbsp water

Do not rinse the Cornish game hens, wipe them with a damp cloth or paper towels. In a small bowl mix garlic with hoisin sauce and brown bean paste.

Heat oil in a saucepan over moderate heat and add the garlic mixture. Cook and stir the mixture in hot oil for 1 minute. Add the Cornish game hens, brown the skin, and coat with the sauce. Add orange peel, wine, soy sauce, salt, sugar, and enough water to cover ⅔ of the birds. Bring to a rapid boil, then cover and cook for 15 to 20 minutes. Turn the birds over once during cooking period. Remove saucepan from heat and let stand for ½ hour. Following instructions on page 13 on how to carve cooked poultry, cut up the Cornish game hens into bite-sized pieces and place them on a serving platter. Boil the sauce in the pan over high heat, reduce it to about 1 cup, and thicken with dissolved cornstarch. Pour sauce over Cornish game hens and serve. Serves 6 to 8.

FRIED MOCK SQUAB

炒
假
白
鴿
松

Many of us probably are living in areas where it would not be easy to obtain such birds as quails and squabs. This version is a close imitation that enables us to experience the delicate flavor of the dish. It is eaten by placing one heaping tablespoonful of the mixture on a piece of lettuce, rolling it up like an egg roll, and eating it with the hands. It is a fun dish to serve to your guests. Besides, it can be cooked in advance and reheated. If squabs are available, replace Chinese sausages and chicken with 12 oz of ground squab.

     2 Chinese sausages
     2 Tbsps oil
     1 tsp minced ginger
     4 Tbsps chopped scallions
    12 oz chopped chicken meat
     1 Tbsp Shao-sing wine, sake, or dry sherry
    ½ Tbsp soy sauce
    ½ tsp sugar
     2 Tbsps oyster sauce
    ½ cup chopped bamboo shoots
    ⅓ cup defrosted frozen peas
     5 Chinese mushrooms, soaked in ¼ cup water for 15
           minutes and finely chopped
    ¼ cup chicken stock
    ½ Tbsp cornstarch dissolved in 1 Tbsp of water
    20 pieces of leaf lettuce or boston lettuce, each about
           5 inches in diameter

Cut or chop Chinese sausages into small pieces. Set a wok or a skillet over moderate heat. When the pan is hot, add sausages. Stir-fry for about 1 minute, then remove fried sausages to a small bowl. Omit this step if squab is used.

Heat oil in a wok or skillet over moderate heat and add ginger and scallions. Stir the two ingredients in hot oil for a few seconds and quickly add the chicken. Stir and cook until it changes color. Add wine and mix well. Add soy sauce, sugar, and oyster sauce and stir and mix everything evenly, then add bamboo shoots, peas, mushrooms, fried Chinese sausages, and chicken stock. Stir and cook everything for 2 minutes, then thicken with dissolved cornstarch. Transfer the whole mixture to a serving plate and serve with lettuce leaves. Serves 4.

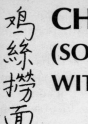

CHICKEN LO-MEIN
(SOFT FRIED NOODLES WITH CHICKEN)

Lo-Mein, a wonderful one-dish meal for lunch or supper, is also one of my favorite dishes for serving at picnics or buffet dinners for 20 to 40 people. It is easy to handle and can be prepared in advance, then reheated in the oven or a microwave oven. This delicious chicken and vegetable version is a winning combination.

4 dried Chinese mushrooms, soaked and cut into thin slivers (optional)
8 oz boned chicken breast
1 tsp Shao-sing wine, sake, or dry sherry
1 tsp cornstarch
1½ Tbsps soy sauce
3 Tbsps oil
½ lb fresh Chinese egg noodles, or ¼ lb dry Chinese egg noodles, or ¼ lb spaghetti
¼ tsp salt or ⅛ tsp salt if oyster sauce is used
2 cups thinly cut cabbage, firmly packed
3 scallions, cut into slivers about 2 inches long
1 Tbsp oyster sauce (optional)
½ cup chicken stock (see page 23)
Black pepper

In a small saucepan cover mushrooms with ½ cup water and simmer over low heat for 15 minutes.

Cut chicken into thin strips about 2 inches long. Mix chicken with 1 tsp wine, 1 tsp cornstarch, ½ Tbsp soy sauce, and ½ Tbsp oil.

Fill a 4-quart saucepan half full of water and bring it to a boil over a high flame. Drop in the noodles and bring to a boil again.

Loosen the noodles in the water with a pair of chopsticks or a fork, cook for 2 minutes, and drain.

Heat ½ Tbsp oil in a wok over high heat. Add ⅛ tsp salt and drop in cabbage. Stir-fry for 2 minutes, then remove to a plate. Pour the remaining oil into the wok, heat until very hot, then add chicken. Stir and separate chicken in the hot oil as it cooks. When chicken becomes white and firm, add scallions, mushrooms, the remaining 1 Tbsp soy sauce, and the oyster sauce or the remaining ⅛ tsp salt, chicken stock, and last, the noodles. Stir and mix noodles thoroughly with the sauce. Sprinkle black pepper evenly over the noodles, then blend in the cabbage. Transfer the mixture to a platter and serve. Serves 4.

STEAMED CHICKEN BUNS WITH BLACK BEAN SAUCE

豉
汁
鸡
饱

1   lb boned chicken, white or dark meat
1   Tbsp Shao-sing wine, sake, or dry sherry
2   Tbsps soy sauce
1   Tbsp cornstarch
5   Tbsps oil
2   Tbsps fermented black beans
1   cup chopped onion
2   Tbsps oyster sauce
1   tsp sugar
¾   cup chicken stock (see page 23)
1½ Tbsps cornstarch dissolved in 2 Tbsps water
1   tsp sesame oil
1   recipe steamed bread dough (see page 88)
    Wax paper cut into 2½-inch squares.

Cut chicken into ½-inch squares about ¼ inch thick. Mix chicken with wine, 1 Tbsp soy sauce, dry cornstarch, and 1 Tbsp oil.

Rinse fermented black beans, then mash them with mortar and pestle.

Heat the remaining oil in a skillet or a wok over high heat. When hot, drop in chicken and stir to separate the pieces. Cook for about 1 minute; with a slotted spoon, remove chicken from pan and drain.

Add onion to the pan and cook until soft and slightly brown. Stir in fermented black bean paste and cook for 15 seconds to bring out the flavor. Add oyster sauce, sugar, stock, and the remaining 1 Tbsp soy sauce. Bring to a boil; thicken with dissolved cornstarch. Mix in cooked chicken and sesame oil.

Transfer to a plate and cool for 6 hours or overnight in the refrigerator.

Roll steamed bread dough into a long sausage-shaped roll about 2 inches in diameter. Cut roll crosswise into 1½-inch sections. Flatten each section with the palm of the hand and then roll the dough out with a rolling pin to about 4 inches in diameter. The center should be a bit thicker than the edges.

Put 1 heaping Tbsp filling in the center of each wrapping. Then gather the edges of the wrapping evenly up over the filling, making a pucker at the top. Twist the peak firmly to seal. Stick a piece of waxed paper on the bottom of each bun. Place buns in steamer and steam for 10 minutes over rapidly boiling water. Serve the buns hot. Cold or frozen buns can be resteamed.

Steamed Bread Dough

 发面

This dough is used as the wrapping for steamed buns. It is also the basis for steamed bread, which in China is eaten plain.

2 tsps dry yeast
½ cup lukewarm water
4½ cups all-purpose flour
2 Tbsps sugar
2 Tbsps shortening
⅔ cup hot water

Dissolve yeast in ½ cup lukewarm water, then stir in ½ cup flour. Set aside for 15 minutes until the yeast bubbles up.

In another cup or bowl dissolve sugar and shortening in the ⅔ cup hot water and let it cool to lukewarm.

Mix 4 cups flour thoroughly with the yeast mixture and the sugar mixture, and knead for about 5 minutes or until dough is smooth. Place dough in a big bowl and cover with a damp towel or a piece of clear plastic wrap. Let it rise until it is double in size (about 2 to 3 hours).

Turn the dough onto a floured surface and knead it again for another 2 minutes until it is smooth and elastic. The dough is now ready to be made into steamed bread or used for wrapping buns.

Note: Ready-made plain biscuit dough can be substituted for home-made bun dough. Biscuit dough is pre-cut to the size of a regular dinner biscuit; being smaller than the bun, it takes less filling.

FUKIEN AND TAIWAN

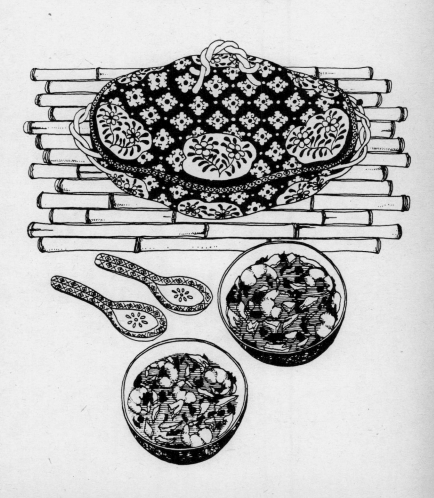

Geographically, the Taiwan Straits separate Fukien from Taiwan, but culturally Fukien is more closely related to Taiwan than to those mainland provinces adjacent to it. The Taiwanese and Fukienese share the same ancestors, speak the same language, and have the same culinary traditions. Their cuisine is called Min cooking. The term *Min* comes from the name of the main river that flows through Fukien Province. A great number of Chinese who reside in the Philippines and all over Southeast Asia are originally from Fukien. Many Filipino dishes and much of Malaysian and Indonesian cooking are clearly influenced by the immigrants from this part of China.

Min cuisine is noted for its large numbers of soups and souplike dishes. In an elaborate ten-course feast, it is not unusual to find that five are in soup form. Because soup dishes play such a major role in Fukien cooking, they have the most exquisite and highly refined broths. Nothing but the best and freshest ingredients are used in making Min soups. The basic stock for Min dishes is made by simmering freshly killed chicken, tasty ham, and lean pork over a low fire for many hours. Another specialty of Min cooking is the fermented red wine lees paste, which is used extensively for flavoring pork and poultry. The recipe for making fermented red wine lees paste is given in this section. A ready-made form is available in some Oriental stores in larger Chinatowns.

Since Fukien is a coastal province and Taiwan is surrounded by water, they have an abundance of fish and seafood. A superb and most refined shrimp sauce and fish sauce are used as important flavoring agents for their soups and many mildly seasoned dishes. Certainly the extensive use of these sauces in southeast Asian cooking must have been introduced by the Fukienese.

To ensure the authenticity of Min cooking, a piece of salty hard ham such as Smithfield is a must for steamed poultry dishes and for the soups. The delicate taste of Smithfield ham adds a most important touch to the entire dish. Ask your butcher to order you either a whole leg of ham or a few pounds of it; the ham will keep for months in the freezer after it is cooked. If you are cooking a whole ham, prepare it according to directions on the wrapping, or steam a small chunk weighing about 1 pound for 1 hour.

紅 FERMENTED RED
糟 WINE LEES PASTE

This recipe is for a modified version of fermented red wine lees paste. The flavor is not as rich as the original version and the consistency is thinner, but it can be made much more quickly and easily. The original fermented red wine lees paste is made by steaming glutinous rice, then mixing it with raw red rice and wine yeast. The rice mixture is then sealed tightly and left undisturbed for 1 month while it undergoes fermentation. After 30 days, the fermented rice is wrapped in cheesecloth and the wine is pressed out. The dry rice lees are again sealed in an urn and the paste is ready for use after 1 year.

Making fermented red wine lees paste requires skill and experience. Chinese do not make it at home. The paste is manufactured by famous companies with their secret recipes. Since authentic fermented red wine lees paste made in Taiwan or the People's Republic of China is not available in the States, I am offering this simplified version.

> 2 Tbsps fermented red bean curd, mashed
> 5 tsps brown sugar
> 1 Tbsp soy sauce
> ½ cup Shao-sing wine or Japanese sake (no other substitute)
> 1 tsp minced ginger
> ½ Tbsp minced garlic
> 1 Tbsp rice flour

In a small saucepan combine all the ingredients and simmer over low heat stirring constantly for 10 minutes. Leftover paste can be kept in the refrigerator for as long as a month in a covered bowl or jar.

紅糟鸡 CHICKEN IN FERMENTED RED WINE LEES PASTE

1 whole chicken breast and 2 chicken legs
2 Tbsps oil
3 Tbsps fermented red wine lees paste (see page 93)
½ tsp sugar (omit sugar if hoisin sauce is used)
2 Tbsps Shao-sing wine, sake, or dry sherry
1 Tbsp soy or hoisin sauce
3 slices of ginger, about 1 inch in diameter
2 scallions, cut into 2-inch sections
½ cup chicken stock, homemade or canned (see page 23)
½ Tbsp sesame oil

Chop chicken meat and bones into 1½-inch pieces.

In a heavy saucepan heat oil over moderate heat. Stir in fermented red wine lees paste and sugar, cook for 30 seconds. Drop in chicken; with a wooden spoon turn the pieces around to coat with the paste. Add wine, soy sauce, ginger, scallions, and stock. Cover pan and simmer over low heat for 20 minutes. Uncover pan and stir in sesame oil. Transfer chicken to a serving plate and serve either hot or cold. Serves 6.

炸块鸡 TAIWAN DEEP-FRIED CHICKEN

    1   small chicken, about 2½ pounds; or chicken breasts
            and legs; or chicken wings
    2   Tbsps Shao-sing wine, sake, or dry sherry
    1   tsp salt
    ⅛   tsp white pepper
    ½   Tbsp minced garlic
    1   Tbsp sesame oil
    1   egg, beaten
    5   Tbsps cornstarch
    4   cups oil
    3   small sprigs of parsley

Rinse chicken and dry thoroughly. Chop chicken into pieces about 1½ inches wide and 2 inches long. In a large bowl marinate chicken with wine, salt, pepper, garlic, and sesame oil for 30 minutes. Mix in egg and cornstarch.

Heat oil in a wok or deep-fryer over moderate heat until hot, about 350°. Divide chicken into two batches and fry first batch for 10 minutes until golden brown. Remove chicken from oil and drain. Repeat with second batch. Place chicken on a platter, garnish with parsley, and serve. Serves 4 to 6.

BRAISED CHICKEN BREAST WITH SCALLIONS

葱
段
生
煎
鸡

Here is a simple and delicious way of enriching the delicate flavor of chicken breast. The coating of egg white and cornstarch helps seal in the juice, keeping the meat tender and moist. In the summer when leeks are in season, replace scallions with leeks for variation.

12 oz boned chicken breast
 1 Tbsp Shao-sing wine, sake, or dry sherry
 ¼ tsp salt
 1 Tbsp cornstarch
 1 egg white
 4 Tbsps oil
 2 cups shredded scallions
 1 Tbsp soy sauce
 ½ tsp sugar
 2 Tbsps chicken stock (see page 23)

Cut chicken into slices about 1 inch wide, 2 inches long, and ¼ · inch thick. Mix chicken with wine, salt, cornstarch, and egg white.

Heat 2 Tbsps oil in a skillet over moderate heat; brown chicken one side at a time until both sides are golden brown. Remove to a plate and repeat with the rest of the chicken.

Add the remaining oil to the skillet, drop in scallions and stir-fry until soft. Add chicken, soy sauce, sugar, and stock. Blend everything together quickly, then transfer to a plate and serve. Serves 4.

STEAMED CHICKEN IN WINE

酒
蒸
鸡

1 whole chicken breast and 2 legs (thighs and
     drumsticks)
6 cups cold water
3 dates
1 cup Shao-sing wine or sake (no other substitute)
3 slices of ginger, 1 inch in diameter
3 scallions, cut into 3-inch sections
½ tsp salt
1 cup hot water
1 piece of wax paper.

With a cleaver, chop chicken up into 2-inch-wide chunks. In a saucepan bring the cold water to boil over high heat. Blanch chicken in boiling water for 3 minutes, then drain.

Put chicken in a lidded casserole; add dates, wine, ginger, scallions, salt, and the hot water. Place wax paper over the top of the casserole and then cover the whole thing with the lid. Place casserole on a rack in a saucepan that is slightly larger than the casserole; add water. Cover pan and steam for 3 hours according to instructions on page 21. Serve the soup directly from the casserole. Serves 6.

CHICKEN AND CUCUMBER SOUP

鸡
片
黄
瓜
汤

6 oz boned chicken breast
¼ tsp salt
½ Tbsp Shao-sing wine, sake, or dry sherry
1 tsp cornstarch
1 cucumber
1 Tbsp oil
4 cups chicken stock, homemade or canned (see page 23)
1 Tbsp light soy sauce
Salt to taste
½ tsp sesame oil

Cut chicken into thin slices according to instructions on page 16. Mix chicken with salt, wine, and cornstarch and set aside.

Peel cucumber and cut in two lengthwise. Scrape out the seeds with a spoon. Cut each half crosswise diagonally into 1- by 2-inch slices.

In a saucepan heat oil over moderate heat, drop in cucumber. Stir cucumber in hot oil for about 1 minute. Pour in stock, cover, and bring to a boil, then lower heat and simmer for 2 minutes. Uncover, add chicken; stir to separate the pieces. Boil soup for a minute, then add salt and sesame oil. Pour into a large bowl and serve hot. Serves 6.

CHICKEN EGG DROP SOUP

鸡
片
蛋
花
汤

This delicious soup is light and refreshing. It is also easy and economical. Cook it hours in advance or put it together in 15 minutes as a last-minute addition to the dinner.

4   oz boned chicken breast
1   Tbsp oil
2   Tbsps chopped scallion
1   medium-sized tomato, diced
½   tsp salt
3   cups chicken stock (see page 23) or water
2   eggs, beaten

Cut chicken into very thin slices about 1-inch square, according to instructions on page 16.

Heat oil in a saucepan over medium heat, add chopped scallion, and stir in hot oil for about 20 seconds. Add tomato and salt; cover until tomato becomes soft. Pour in stock or water and bring to a rapid boil. Cover pan and boil soup for 5 minutes.

Uncover pan, add chicken, and bring the soup to a boil. Turn off heat, then stir in the egg slowly, a tablespoonful at a time. When egg is set, transfer soup into a serving bowl and serve hot. Serves 4.

CHICKEN RICE PORRIDGE

鸡
美

Rice porridge, rice gruel, or congee, whatever it may be called, is a soupy soft rice made by simmering rice in water over a long period of time. The water ration in making rice porridge is considerably more than the amount of water for cooking regular rice. The consistency of rice porridge varies from region to region. This recipe is a thinner version, an ideal soup for a buffet dinner in the winter.

Rice porridge is eaten throughout China at breakfast, at midnight, or as a between-meal snack. For centuries it has been the baby food of China. Since rice porridge is easily digestible, it is also a popular food to serve to a sick person.

> 3 Tbsps rice, either long grain or short grain
> 1 Tbsp glutinous rice
> ¼ cup raw peanuts
> 1 Tbsp of small dried shrimp or 2 Tbsps chopped
>   Smithfield ham
> 4 cups water
> 3 oz boned chicken breast
> ½ Tbsp Shao-sing wine, or sake, or dry sherry
> 1 tsp cornstarch
> ½ tsp salt
> 1 Tbsp light soy sauce
> 1 tsp sesame oil
>   Dash white or black pepper
> 1 Tbsp finely chopped scallion

In a large saucepan combine rice, glutinous rice, peanuts, and dried shrimp or Smithfield ham with the water and bring to a boil over high heat. Cover the pan, reduce the heat to very low, and simmer for 1 hour.

Slice chicken into very thin pieces, about 1 inch square, according to instructions on page 16. Mix chicken with wine and cornstarch. Set aside.

When the rice is ready, add chicken and bring to a boil. Stir in salt, soy sauce, sesame oil, and pepper. Garnish with chopped scallion and serve hot. Serves 6 to 8.

蔴油鴐汤 CHICKEN AND SESAME OIL SOUP

This soup is light yet very rich in flavor. It is simple to prepare and, when boiled noodles are added, makes a hearty one-dish meal.

> ½ chicken or two legs, about 1½ lbs
> 2 Tbsps sesame oil
> 3 slices ginger, about 1 inch in diameter
> ½ cup Shao-sing wine or sake (no other substitute)
> 2½ cups boiling water
> 1 tsp salt
> ½ tsp sugar

Chop chicken meat and bones into 1½-inch pieces, according to instructions on page 13.

In a saucepan heat sesame oil over moderate heat. Add ginger and cook for 20 seconds; drop in chicken and brown for 2 minutes. Add wine and bring to a rolling boil, then add the boiling water, salt, and sugar. Cover and simmer over a low fire for 30 minutes. This soup can be prepared in advance and reheated. Serves 4 to 6.

CHICKEN AND SHRIMP SOUP

鸡
肉
虾
仁
汤

The shrimp in the recipe can be replaced with the same amount of crab meat, or omitted for a more economical dish.

> 4   oz boned chicken breast
> 1   tsp cornstarch
> 1   tsp soy sauce
> 1   Tbsp oil
> 1   tsp minced ginger
> 3   cups chicken stock, homemade (see page 00) or canned
> ½   Tbsp Shao-sing wine, or sake, or dry sherry
> 4   medium-sized shrimp, shelled and each one split in two
> 2   cups fresh spinach, washed and broken into small pieces
> ½   tsp salt (omit salt if canned stock is used)
>   Dash black pepper
> 1   tsp sesame oil

Cut chicken into thin slivers according to instructions on page 16. In a small bowl mix chicken with cornstarch and soy sauce.

Heat oil in a saucepan over moderate heat, add ginger, and stir for 10 seconds. Pour in stock and wine and bring to a boil. Add chicken and shrimp, stirring to separate the chicken slivers. Boil soup for 1 minute. Add spinach, salt, pepper, and sesame oil. Transfer to a soup tureen. Serves 4 to 6.

鸡
火
龙
须
汤 CHICKEN AND HAM WITH ASPARAGUS SOUP

- 6 oz boned chicken breast
- ½ Tbsp Shao-sing wine, sake, or dry sherry
- ¾ tsp salt
- 1 tsp cornstarch
- 3 cups chicken stock, homemade (see page 23) or canned
- 1 cup thinly sliced fresh asparagus
- ¼ cup thinly sliced cooked Smithfield ham
- ½ tsp sesame oil

Follow the instructions on page 16, slice chicken into thin pieces about ⅛ inch thick and 1 inch square. Mix chicken with wine, ¼ tsp salt, and the cornstarch.

In a saucepan bring chicken stock and asparagus to a boil; add chicken, stirring to separate the pieces. Add ham and boil for 1 minute, then stir in sesame oil and the remaining salt. Transfer to a bowl and serve. Serves 4 to 6.

CHICKEN FEET AND MUSHROOM SOUP

冬
菇
鸡
脚
汤

Because chicken feet supply a good amount of natural gelatin, the Chinese for centuries have considered them a nutritious food and rank them with parts such as livers, gizzards, and intestines as great delicacies. As you can see in this recipe, the chicken feet are paired with expensive ingredients like dried black mushrooms.

> 16 dried Chinese black mushrooms, about 1½ inches in diameter
> 12 chicken feet
> 4 cups water
> 1 Tbsp Shao-sing wine, sake, or dry sherry
> Salt to taste

Rinse mushrooms in cold water, then cover them with 1 cup warm water and let stand for 30 minutes. Remove and discard stems, but reserve the soaking liquid.

Rinse chicken feet thoroughly and remove the layer of waxy skin. Cut off the sharp nails.

Put chicken feet, mushrooms, and soaking liquid in a heavy saucepan; add water and the wine. Bring to a rolling boil, then cover tightly and simmer over very low heat for 1½ hours. Add salt to taste and serve. Serves 4 to 6.

CHICKEN LIVER AND SPINACH SOUP

鸡
肝
菠
菜
汤

The combination of chicken livers and spinach makes an unbelievably delicious soup. Even if you are a liver-hater, you'll like the broth.

 5 pairs of fresh chicken livers
½ Tbsp soy sauce
 1 tsp cornstarch
 1 tsp oil
 3 cups chicken stock (see page 23) or water
 3 cups fresh spinach, rinsed and cut into 1-inch-wide
      pieces
    Salt to taste

Rinse chicken livers. Cut each pair into halves, then cut each half crosswise into ½-inch-thick pieces. Mix liver with soy sauce, cornstarch, and oil.

In a saucepan bring stock or water to a boil, add chicken livers and spinach. Return to boil for 30 seconds, season with salt, transfer to a soup tureen and serve. Serves 4 to 6.

红工
糟片鸭
FRIED DUCK WITH FERMENTED RED WINE LEES PASTE

I am sure you will enjoy this dish. Though it is slightly complicated, it can be prepared in advance. The taste becomes richer
when the finished dish is set for a day or two in the refrigerator.
Allow the duck to warm to room temperature before it is
served.

When duck is served in Western style it is often a problem to
extend the number of servings. Prepared in the Chinese way—
particularly in this recipe in which the duck is boned and cut up
into small pieces—it provides generous portions for 6 to 8
people.

> 20 cups water
> 1 duck, about 4 lbs
> 2 cups oil
> 4 scallions, cut into 2-inch sections
> 6 slices of ginger, about 1 inch in diameter
> 4 Tbsps fermented red wine lees paste (see page 93)
>   or hoisin sauce
> 2 Tbsps Shao-sing wine, sake, or dry sherry
> 2 cups chicken stock (see page 23)
> 2 Tbsps cornstarch
> 2 egg whites, slightly beaten
> 4 Tbsps flour

In a large saucepan bring 20 cups of water to a boil. Put the
duck into the boiling water and blanch for 5 minutes, remove
duck from water, and drain; discard the water.

Heat 4 Tbsps oil in a wok over moderate heat. Drop in scallions
and ginger, stir-fry until the scallions become soft. Add fermented red wine lees paste or hoisin sauce, stir and cook 20

seconds. Add wine and chicken stock and bring to a boil. Place the duck into the pan, simmer covered for 1 hour, then cool the duck thoroughly in the sauce.

Cut duck into 4 quarters, then remove all the bones according to the instructions on page 14, leaving the wings unboned. Dust each quarter thoroughly and generously with cornstarch.

In a mixing bowl combine egg whites and flour to form a batter.

Heat the remaining oil in a wok over moderate heat until oil is hot. Coat each quarter of duck with the batter, deep-fry two pieces at a time for about 2 to 3 minutes, and drain. Repeat with the other two pieces of duck. Cut each piece, hot or chilled, into 4 equal portions, place them on a plate, and serve. Serves 6 to 8.

咸菜鴨汤 DUCK SOUP WITH SOUR MUSTARD GREENS

Ducks sold in the United States are rather fat. To prevent the soup from becoming too oily, remove duck skin and fat before cooking. Chicken can be used in place of duck; however the broth will not have the nice gamey flavor of the duck.

> ½ duck
> 4 cups water
> 1 cup sliced sour mustard greens (see below)
> ½ tsp salt
> 1 tsp sesame oil

Cut duck crosswise into 2 pieces, simmer duck with water until tender. Transfer duck to plate and bone it, according to instructions on page 14. Then cut the meat into bite-sized pieces and set aside. Add sour mustard greens to duck broth and boil for 2 minutes. Add the duck meat, salt, and sesame oil. Transfer to a soup bowl and serve hot. Serves 4 to 6.

Sour Mustard Greens

The best sour mustard greens I have ever eaten are made by the Swatow people of Kwangtung Province. Home-made sour mustard greens are far superior to the commercial variety. The following recipe for sour mustard greens was given to me by my Swatow relatives. Stored in the refrigerator, these mustard greens will keep indefinitely.

In order to obtain a crunchy texture, the vegetables must be blanched in boiling water and then rinsed thoroughly with cold water. Be sure the vegetables and the container are free of grease.

   3 *lbs broad-leaf mustard greens*
  13 *cups water*
  ¼ *cup salt*
   1 *cup sugar*
  ½ *cup white vinegar*
   1 *tsp dried chili pepper flakes, if desired*
   1 *Tbsp Shao-sing wine, sake, or dry sherry*

Wash mustard greens thoroughly, cut into 1-inch by 2-inch pieces.

In a saucepan, bring 10 cups of water to a boil. Drop in mustard greens and blanch for 30 seconds. Remove from hot water and rinse immediately with cold water until greens are cool, then drain well.

In a saucepan bring salt, sugar, vinegar, and the remaining 3 cups of water to a boil, then cool.

Rinse a glass container with the wine and wipe dry with paper towels. Place mustard greens in the container, add chili flakes, and pour in salt mixture. Press down the greens with a clean spoon, making sure they are completely immersed in the solution. Set aside for 2 days uncovered. Cover and store in the refrigerator. Makes 3 cups.

鴨腸炒芹菜 STIR-FRIED DUCK INTESTINES WITH CELERY

Because of their crunchy texture and limited supply, both duck intestines and goose intestines are highly prized by the Chinese. Thinly sliced chicken and duck gizzards can be substituted for duck intestines if they are not available. Clean and cut up the gizzards following the instructions in the recipe for Chicken Gizzards and Watercress Egg Drop Soup (page 70), then cook without soaking or blanching.

> 12 oz duck intestines
> 1 Tbsp salt
> 1 tsp baking soda
> 10 cups water
> ½ Tbsp Shao-sing wine, sake, or dry sherry
> 1 Tbsp light soy sauce
> ¼ tsp sugar
> ¼ tsp salt
> 2 Tbsps oil
> 2 cups sliced celery, about 2 inches long
> 1 Tbsp chopped fresh chili pepper or 1 tsp dried red
>   pepper flakes

With a sharp paring knife, split open the whole length of the intestines, remove and discard fat, if any, rub with salt thoroughly, and rinse well. Cut into 2-inch lengths. Dissolve baking soda in 6 cups of water and soak intestines in the solution for 15 minutes, then rinse well. Bring the remaining water to boil and blanch the intestines in hot water for 1 minute and drain. (If chicken or duck gizzards are used, omit this step.)

In a small bowl, combine wine, soy sauce, sugar, and salt.

Heat 1 Tbsp oil in wok or a skillet over high heat. Add celery and stir-fry for 30 seconds. Transfer to a plate. Heat the remaining oil until hot; add the chili pepper and intestines. Toss and cook for 30 seconds, add the wine mixture and the celery, and blend together. Transfer to a serving plate and serve at once. Serves 4.

蒸白鸽汤 STEAMED PIGEON SOUP

  6 dried Chinese black mushrooms
  2 pigeons, about 12 oz each
 10 cups water
  1 Tbsp Shao-sing wine, sake, or dry sherry
  2 slices of ginger, about 1 inch in diameter
  2 scallions, cut into 2-inch sections
  4 oz Smithfield ham, thinly sliced
  4 cups chicken stock, homemade (see page 23) or
       canned
    Salt to taste

Soak mushrooms in ½ cup hot water for 30 minutes. Remove and discard mushroom stems and cut each cap in half.

Cut each pigeon into quarters. In a large saucepan bring water to boil, blanch pigeons for 1 minute, and drain.

Place pigeons in a deep bowl, add wine, mushrooms, ginger, scallions, ham, and chicken stock or water. Steam for 2 hours according to instructions on page 21.

Remove the bowl containing the pigeon soup from the steamer, discard ginger and scallions. Season with salt and serve hot. This dish can be prepared in advance and reheated. Serves 6 to 8.

HUNAN

Traditionally, Hunan food is not classified among the major schools of Chinese cooking. Because of its spicy dishes, it is often listed as a subgroup under the cooking of Szechuan. However, in the past decade its rapid gain in popularity both at home and abroad has given Hunan cooking separate recognition. Moreover, Hunan is the home province of the late Chairman Mao Tse-tung, so much attention has been focused on this province. In Mao's rise, his influence on the nation extended to the gastronomic.

The two most outstanding features of Hunan cooking are peppery dishes and smoked salt-cured meats. To prevent spoilage, meat and poultry are salted and smoked, then hung in the air to dry. Because a great part of Hunan is low country with rather warm and humid weather, the inhabitants of the area believe hot peppers have the pharmacological effect of giving heat to the body, hence helping to cure rheumatism caused by the dampness.

In addition to peppers, vinegar and fermented black beans are also indispensable flavoring items. Hunan cuisine can be described as spicy, slightly oily, rich in flavor, dark in color, and soft in texture. It is a common belief among the Chinese that the spicy Hunan diet contributes to the reputed fiery temperament of the Hunan people. I once hired a Hunanese woman to help me with my household chores when I was living in Taiwan. Whenever she had an argument with someone, she went through a very dramatic screaming scene. One time when she threatened to kill herself by beating her head against a stone wall, my neighbors attributed her behavior to her diet. Whatever the reasons, I finally and reluctantly had to give up her good cooking in order to preserve peace in the neighborhood.

东安鸡 DUNG AN CHICKEN
(HUNAN HOT AND SOUR CHICKEN)

This chicken dish is named after the town in Hunan Province where it originated. Because of its unique flavoring it has become a popular dish throughout China, especially loved by enthusiasts of spicy food. When poaching the chicken, do not overcook it.

        1   fryer chicken, about 2 lbs, or 1 whole chicken breast
                and 2 legs
        2   slices of fresh ginger
        2   scallions
        2   Tbsps Shao-sing wine, sake, or dry sherry
        2   Tbsps oil
        2   Tbsps fresh hot chili peppers or 1 tsp dry pepper
                flakes
        2   Tbsps finely shredded fresh ginger
        4   scallions, shredded
        2   cloves of garlic, crushed
        2   Tbsps soy sauce
       ¼   tsp salt
        1   tsp sugar
        2   Tbsps wine vinegar
       ½   tsp Szechuan peppercorn powder (see page 40)
        1   cup chicken stock (see page 23)
       ½   Tbsp cornstarch, dissolved in 1 Tbsp water
        1   tsp sesame oil

Wash chicken and put it in a saucepan just big enough to hold it. Pour in 3 or 4 cups of water, enough to just cover the chicken. Add sliced ginger, scallions, and 1 Tbsp wine. Set saucepan over moderate heat, bring water to boil, cover pan, and cook for 20 minutes.

Remove chicken from water, drain, and cool. Put chicken on a chopping board and cut into 2-inch squares.

Set a wok or a skillet over high heat, add oil, chili pepper, shredded ginger, shredded scallion, and garlic. Stir the ingredients in hot oil for a few seconds, drop in chicken, and stir-fry for about 15 seconds. Add soy sauce, 1 Tbsp wine, salt, sugar, vinegar, peppercorn powder, and stock, then thicken sauce with dissolved cornstarch. Add sesame oil. Transfer chicken to a plate and serve. Serves 6.

BRAISED CHICKEN AND MUSHROOMS

10 medium-sized Chinese mushrooms
 1 cup hot water
 1 chicken, about 2½ pounds, or 1 chicken breast with
     ribs and 2 chicken legs
 3 Tbsps soy sauce
 3 Tbsps oil
 2 slices of fresh ginger
 3 scallions, cut into 2-inch sections
 3 Tbsps Shao-sing wine, sake, or dry sherry
 ½ tsp salt
 1 tsp sugar
 1 cup chicken stock (see page 23) or water
 ½ Tbsp cornstarch dissolved in 2 Tbsps water
 1 Tbsp sesame oil

Soak mushrooms in hot water for 30 minutes. Rinse off sand, remove and discard stems. Cut each cap in two.

Wash chicken and dry well with paper towels. Cut chicken into 1-inch by 2-inch pieces. In a bowl mix chicken with 1 Tbsp soy sauce.

Set a heavy saucepan on medium heat and pour in oil. When oil is hot, add ginger and scallions, stir for a few seconds, then add chicken. Stir-fry chicken until outside becomes firm and slightly brown, add wine, salt, sugar, the remaining soy sauce, and the stock and mushrooms. Bring to a boil and cover the pan. Lower the heat and let simmer for 30 to 40 minutes. Thicken sauce with dissolved cornstarch and stir in sesame oil. Transfer to a plate and serve. This dish can be prepared in advance and re-heated. Serves 6.

COLD CHICKEN WITH CHILI PEPPER OIL SAUCE

辣
油
嫩
鸡

1 chicken, about 1½ lb, or 1 whole breast with rib
    bones, or ½ chicken, or 2 legs
1 Tbsp sesame oil
2 Tbsps finely chopped scallion
2 Tbsps soy sauce
1 Tbsp cider vinegar
½ tsp sugar
½ Tbsp chili pepper oil (see page 30)
¼ cup chicken stock (see page 23)

Rinse chicken, then place it in a pot that fits nicely. Add water to cover 2/3 of the chicken and bring to boil. Cover pot and reduce heat. Simmer for 25 minutes. Remove chicken from stock and cool.

Bone chicken according to instructions on page 14. Cut chicken into ½-inch by 1½-inch pieces; arrange them neatly on a plate.

In a small saucepan or a wok, heat sesame oil; add scallion and cook for 10 seconds, then add the rest of the ingredients and bring to a boil. Pour the sauce over chicken and serve. Serves 4.

酸辣鸡丁 HOT AND SOUR DICED CHICKEN

Sour and peppery flavor is the main feature of Hunanese cooking. The spiciness of this dish is rather mild by Hunanese standards, so add more red pepper flakes if you like hot food.

12 oz boned chicken meat, white or dark
½ Tbsp Shao-sing wine, sake, or dry sherry
2 Tbsps soy sauce
1 Tbsp cornstarch
1 small egg white
1 Tbsp vinegar
¼ tsp sugar
¼ cup chicken stock (see page 23)
½ Tbsp sesame oil
1 cup oil (see page 20 on stir-frying)
½ cup chopped scallions
1 tsp minced garlic
1 Tbsp minced fresh chili pepper or 1 tsp dried red pepper flakes
½ cup coarsely chopped sour mustard greens (see page 108), or commercial pickled cucumber

Dice chicken, then mix with wine, 1 Tbsp soy sauce, and the cornstarch and egg white.

In a small bowl combine vinegar, sugar, stock, sesame oil, and the remaining soy sauce.

Heat oil in a wok over moderate heat until hot but not smoking, then drop in chicken. Stir to separate meat, and cook for 1 to 2 minutes until meat becomes firm. With a slotted spoon, remove chicken from oil and drain.

Empty all but I Tbsp oil from wok; stir-fry scallions, garlic, and chili pepper in oil over high heat for 30 seconds. Add sour mustard greens or pickled cucumber. Toss for 20 seconds, then return chicken to pan and mix in the sauce from the bowl. Transfer to a plate and serve. This dish can be prepared in advance and reheated in the microwave oven. Serves 4.

BRAISED SPICY CHICKEN OR TURKEY WITH BLACK BEAN SAUCE

豆豉辣椒鸡

2 lb chicken or turkey with bone or 1 lb chicken or
    turkey meat
2 Tbsps oil
1 Tbsp chopped fresh hot chili pepper or ½ Tbsp
    dried red pepper flakes
3 Tbsps chopped scallion
2 Tbsps fermented black beans, rinsed
1 Tbsp Shao-sing wine, sake, or dry sherry
2 Tbsps soy sauce
1 tsp sugar
½ cup chicken stock (see page 23) or water

Cut chicken or turkey into 1½-inch cubes.

Heat oil in a wok or a heavy saucepan over moderate heat; add
chili pepper, scallion, black beans. Stir them in hot oil for 30
seconds. Drop in chicken. With a wooden spoon or spatula,
turn the pieces around and coat them with the pepper, scallion,
and black beans. Blend in wine, soy sauce, and sugar, then add
stock or water. Cover saucepan and simmer over low heat for 20
minutes. Transfer chicken to a plate and serve. This dish can be
prepared in advance and reheated. Serves 4 to 6.

STEAMED CHICKEN WITH GARLIC SAUCE

蒸
鸡
块
蒜
瓣

1 lb boned chicken, either white or dark meat
1 Tbsp Shao-sing wine, sake, or dry sherry
¼ tsp salt
1 Tbsp cornstarch
2 Tbsps oil
1 Tbsp sliced garlic
3 Tbsps chopped scallion
2 Tbsps soy sauce
¼ tsp sugar
1 tsp sesame oil

Cut chicken into 1-inch squares. Mix chicken with wine, salt, and cornstarch. In a shallow bowl arrange chicken in one layer and steam according to instructions on page 21 for 10 minutes.

Heat oil in a small saucepan until hot; stir in garlic and cook until it turns slightly brown. Add scallions and cook for 20 seconds. Remove from heat and mix in the rest of the ingredients. Pour sauce over chicken and serve hot. Serves 4 to 6.

CHICKEN CUTLETS WITH PEPPERCORN POWDER

佳
盐
鸡
片

1 lb boned chicken breast
1 Tbsp Shao-sing wine, sake, or dry sherry
½ tsp salt
2 large eggs, beaten
4 Tbsps flour
4 Tbsps cornstarch
1 cup oil
3 Tbsps chopped scallion
½ tsp Szechuan peppercorn powder (see page 40)
1 tsp sesame oil

Cut chicken into slices 1 inch wide by 2 inches long and ¼ inch thick. Marinate in wine and salt for 15 minutes.

In a small bowl mix egg, flour, and cornstarch into a batter. Add chicken and coat each piece thoroughly with batter.

Heat oil in a wok over moderate heat until very hot. Fry 5 or 6 pieces of chicken at a time until golden brown. Remove from oil and drain; repeat with the remaining chicken.

Empty all but ½ Tbsp oil from wok, drop in scallion, stir and cook for 30 seconds or until soft. Blend in fried chicken, then sprinkle with peppercorn powder and sesame oil. Transfer to a plate and serve at once. Serves 4 to 6.

PEPPERS STUFFED WITH CHICKEN

鸡
肉
酿
辣
椒

Traditionally, hot peppers are used for this dish, but either hot or mild fresh peppers make perfect containers for the stuffing. If you like spicy food, you will enjoy the extra biting flavor of the hot chili peppers. Some chili peppers are very hot; wash your hands with soap and water after handling them. The peppers for this dish should be about 4 to 5 inches long and 1½ inches in diameter at the top. The other end can have the same diameter or taper to a narrow point.

 5 dried Chinese black mushrooms, soaked 15 minutes
     in ½ cup warm water
 8 oz ground chicken, preferably dark meat or ½ dark
     and ½ white
 ½ Tbsp Shao-sing wine, sake, or dry sherry
 2 Tbsps chopped scallion
1½ Tbsps soy sauce
 3 tsps cornstarch
 1 small egg, beaten
 9 peppers, 1 to 1½ inches in diameter
 1 Tbsp fermented black beans
 2 Tbsps oil
 1 tsp minced garlic
 ½ cup chicken stock (see page 23)
 ¼ tsp sugar
 1 tsp cornstarch dissolved in 1 Tbsp water
 ½ tsp sesame oil

Remove and discard stems from mushrooms and chop up the caps.

In a bowl, mix chicken with wine, scallion, ½ Tbsp soy sauce, 1 tsp cornstarch, and the egg and mushrooms.

Cut each pepper lengthwise into two equal halves, remove and discard the stems and seeds. Stuff each half with the chicken mixture, then sprinkle the remaining dry cornstarch over the meat.

Rinse the black beans with cold water and crush into a paste with mortar and pestle, or put the beans in a small bowl and pound them with the handle of a cleaver.

Heat 1 Tbsp oil in a skillet over moderate heat and brown the stuffed peppers, with the meat side facing down, for 2 minutes. Place them on a plate with the meat side facing up. Put aside the skillet for later use.

Steam peppers for 10 minutes according to instructions on page 21. Heat skillet over medium heat, add the remaining oil, then stir in garlic and black beans; cook for 15 seconds. Add stock, the remaining soy sauce, the sugar, and the juices from the steamed peppers; bring to a boil. Thicken sauce with the dissolved cornstarch and stir in sesame oil. Pour sauce over peppers and serve. This dish can be prepared in advance and reheated. Serves 4.

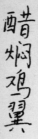

BRAISED SPICY CHICKEN WINGS WITH VINEGAR

10 chicken wings
 8 cups water
¼ cup cider or wine vinegar
½ Tbsp dried chili pepper flakes
 2 Tbsps Shao-sing wine, sake, or dry sherry
 2 slices of ginger, about 1 inch in diameter
¼ tsp salt
 1 Tbsp soy sauce
½ tsp sugar

Rinse chicken wings and dry with paper towels. Chop off and discard the tip of each chicken wing; cut the remaining sections apart at the joint.

In a saucepan, bring water to a boil; drop in chicken wings, and blanch for 2 minutes; drain. Put chicken back into the saucepan, add all the rest of the ingredients. Cover pan and simmer over low heat for 15 minutes. This dish can be prepared in advance and reheated. Serves 4.

STIR-FRIED SPICY CHICKEN LIVERS WITH LEEKS

蒜
爆
鸡
肝

10 oz chicken livers
½ Tbsp Shao-sing wine, sake, or dry sherry
1 Tbsp cornstarch
1 Tbsp soy sauce
¼ tsp sugar
3 Tbsps chicken stock (see page 23) or water
½ Tbsp sesame oil
1 cup oil
3 cups sliced leeks
¼ tsp salt
1 Tbsp chopped fresh chili peppers

Rinse chicken livers and drain until very dry. Slice each one into thin pieces about ¼ inch thick. Mix livers with wine and cornstarch.

In a small bowl combine soy sauce, sugar, chicken stock, and sesame oil.

Heat oil in a wok over moderate heat. When oil is hot, drop in livers and cook for 2 minutes. (Caution: When deep-frying chicken livers, protect your arms from oil splatter by wearing long sleeves and standing a couple of feet away from the pan.) Remove livers with a slotted spoon and drain. Empty all but 1 Tbsp oil from wok and reserve the oil, add leeks and salt; stir-fry over moderate heat until leeks become soft. Remove to a plate.

Put Tbsp reserved oil into the pan, stir in chili peppers, and cook for 20 seconds. Add chicken livers, mixture from the bowl, and leeks. Blend thoroughly, transfer to a plate, and serve. Serves 4.

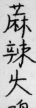

SPICY TURKEY WITH SESAME OIL

Turkey is not just for Thanksgiving anymore, nor just for roasting either. I find preparing turkey meat in the Chinese way surpasses the regular Western cooking methods.

1 lb boned turkey breast
1 Tbsp Shao-sing wine, sake, or dry sherry
3 Tbsps soy sauce
3 Tbsps cornstarch
1 Tbsp vinegar
1 Tbsp sesame oil
½ tsp sugar
2 cups oil
3 Tbsps coarsely chopped fresh chili pepper
½ tsp Szechuan peppercorns, crushed
¼ cup chopped garlic leaves or scallions

Dice turkey into ½-inch cubes. Mix with wine, 1 Tbsp soy sauce, and cornstarch.

In a small bowl, combine the remaining soy sauce with vinegar, sesame oil, and sugar.

Heat oil in a wok over moderate heat to 375°. Drop in turkey and stir to separate meat; cook for 1 minute. With a slotted spoon or a strainer, scoop up turkey. Heat oil until it is very hot again. Return turkey to hot oil and fry for 2 more minutes until it is golden brown. Remove turkey from oil and drain.

Empty all but 1 Tbsp oil from wok. Set the wok over high heat; stir chili pepper and Szechuan peppercorns in hot oil for 15 seconds. Add garlic leaves or scallions, turkey, and soy sauce mixture; stir and blend everything evenly. Transfer to a plate and serve at once. Serves 4 to 6.

STIR-FRIED SMOKED DUCK OR TURKEY

Quite unlike other stir-fried poultry dishes, in this typical Hunanese dish the meat is first smoked and then stir-fried. Any preserved meat can be cooked in this fashion. Vegetables with low water content such as celery, carrots, green peppers, or broccoli are ideal accompanying ingredients with the meat.

    2   Tbsps oil
    1   cup thinly sliced celery
    ⅛   tsp salt
    1   tsp minced ginger
    1   cup sliced smoked duck or smoked turkey (see
           page 19 on smoking)
    ½   Tbsp soy sauce (optional)
    ¼   tsp sugar (omit if soy sauce is not used)
    1   tsp sesame oil

Heat 1 Tbsp oil in a wok or skillet over moderate heat, drop in celery, and stir-fry for 30 seconds. Blend in salt and transfer celery to a plate.

Heat the remaining oil, stir in ginger, and cook for 10 seconds. Add duck or turkey, give it a few tosses, then stir in soy sauce and sugar. Add cooked celery and sesame oil, mix everything thoroughly. Transfer to a plate and serve. Serves 4.

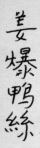

STIR-FRIED SPICY DUCK WITH GINGER

Although roast or braised duck meat usually is used for this dish, I find leftover roast turkey or cooked chicken make a perfect variation on the theme.

    2 Tbsps oil
    ½ cup shredded leeks or scallions
    2 Tbsps chopped fresh chili peppers, with seeds
         removed
    1 cup firmly packed coarsely torn cooked duck meat
    2 Tbsps finely shredded young tender ginger or
         pickled Japanese ginger
    ¼ cup carrot, cut into very thin slivers
    1 Tbsp Shao-sing wine, sake, or dry sherry
  1½ Tbsps soy sauce
    ¼ tsp sugar
    ½ cup celery, cut into thin slivers about 2 inches long
    1 cup fresh bean sprouts (optional)
    1 Tbsp vinegar
    1 tsp sesame oil

Heat oil in a wok or a skillet over high heat; add leeks or scallions and chili peppers. Stir-fry for 1 minute, mix in duck meat, ginger, carrot, wine, soy sauce, and sugar. With a spatula, toss everything for about 1 more minute, then blend in celery, bean sprouts, vinegar, and sesame oil. Mix well and transfer to a plate. Serves 4.

STIR-FRIED SPICY WILD DUCK

酸
辣
野
鴨
片

    12 oz wild duck meat
    ½   Tbsp soy sauce
    ¼   tsp salt
    ½   Tbsp cornstarch
    1   small egg white
    1   cup oil (see page 20 on stir-frying)
    1   tsp minced garlic
    ½   Tbsp dried red pepper flakes
    ¼   cup chopped sour pickles
    1   Tbsp cider vinegar
    ¼   cup sliced water chestnuts
    2   Tbsps chopped scallion
    ¼   cup chicken stock (see page 23)
    1   tsp cornstarch dissolved in 1 Tbsp water
    1   tsp sesame oil

Following instructions on page 16, cut wild duck meat into thin slices about 1 inch wide, 1½ inch long, and ⅛ inch thick. Mix duck with soy sauce, salt, dry cornstarch, and egg white.

Heat oil in a wok over moderate heat until hot but not smoking. Drop in duck, stir to separate the pieces, and cook for 2 minutes. With a slotted spoon, remove duck meat from oil and drain.

Empty all but 1 Tbsp oil from wok; set wok over moderate heat. Add garlic and pepper flakes and stir them in hot oil for 30 seconds to bring out the flavor.

Add pickles, vinegar, water chestnuts, scallion, cooked duck, and stock; blend thoroughly. Mix in dissolved cornstarch and cook until sauce is thickened, about 30 seconds. Sprinkle with sesame oil, transfer to a plate, and serve. Serves 4.

CRISPY PIGEON

香
酥
斑
鳩

Pigeons have a very delicate flavor; they should not be overcooked. After the birds are poached in the seasoned soy sauce, they can be kept uncovered in the refrigerator overnight and then deep-fried just before serving.

11 cups water
2 pigeons, about 12 oz each
3 Tbsps Shao-sing wine, sake, or dry sherry
4 Tbsps soy sauce
1 tsp sugar
½ tsp salt
¼ tsp Szechuan peppercorns
4 slices of ginger, about 1 inch in diameter
4 scallions, cut into 3-inch sections
3 cups oil
1 tsp sesame oil
¼ tsp Szechuan peppercorn powder (see page 40)

In a large saucepan, bring 10 cups water to a boil. Blanch pigeons in boiling water for 2 minutes. Transfer pigeons to a smaller pan just large enough to hold them snugly. Add wine, soy sauce, sugar, salt, Szechuan peppercorns, ginger, scallions, and the remaining water. Bring to a boil over high heat, then cover pan and simmer over low heat with the surface of water barely trembling for 30 minutes. Remove pigeons from stock and discard the stock. Place pigeons in a colander with the tail ends facing down; drain and cool for at least 2 hours.

Heat oil in a wok or deep-fryer over moderate heat until hot but not smoking. Fry pigeons until golden brown (2 to 3 minutes). Remove them from oil and drain. Chop into serving size pieces according to instructions on page 13. Sprinkle with sesame oil and Szechuan peppercorn powder and serve warm. Serves 4 to 6.

蘇油鴿 HUNAN SESAME PIGEON OR CORNISH HEN

2 pigeons about 12 oz each, or 1 Cornish hen
4 Tbsps soy sauce
2 Tbsps Shao-sing wine, sake, or dry sherry
½ tsp sugar
2 scallions, cut into 2-inch sections
4 slices of ginger, crushed
2 Tbsp sesame oil
1 tsp red pepper flakes

Marinate pigeons with soy sauce, wine, sugar, scallions, and ginger for 1 hour.

Place pigeons and the marinade in a bowl and steam for 20 minutes according to instructions on page 21.

Discard ginger and scallions, cut pigeons into serving pieces, according to instructions on page 13, then arrange the pieces on a warm plate.

In a small saucepan, heat sesame oil and add red pepper flakes. Stir and cook over low heat for 2 minutes. Strain, pour the oil over squabs, and serve. Serves 4 to 6.

SPICY CHICKEN AND MUSHROOM SOUP

鸡
片
鲜
菇
汤

This simple and tasty soup can be served either spicy or nonspicy. The slippery mung bean noodles provide extra body and bind the chicken and mushrooms together. It can be prepared hours in advance and reheated.

    2 oz thin dried mung bean noodles
    6 oz chicken meat, white or dark
    ¼ Tbsp Shao-sing wine, sake, or dry sherry
    ½ Tbsp soy sauce
    1 tsp cornstarch
    1 Tbsp oil
    3 Tbsps chopped scallion
    ½ Tbsp brown bean paste (optional)
    4 cups chicken stock (see page 23)
    2 cups sliced fresh mushrooms
    ⅔ tsp salt
       Dash black pepper
    ½ Tbsp hot chili pepper oil (see page 30)
    ½ tsp sesame oil

Soak mung bean noodles in 4 cups of water for 20 minutes. With a pair of scissors, cut them randomly into shorter pieces.

According to instructions on page 16, cut chicken into thin slices, about 1 inch square. Mix chicken with wine, soy sauce, and cornstarch.

Heat oil in a saucepan over moderate heat; stir in scallion and cook until it becomes slightly brown. Add bean paste. Stir in hot oil for 10 seconds, then pour in chicken stock and add mung bean noodles. Bring soup to a boil, cover pan, and simmer for 5 minutes. Uncover pan, add chicken, stirring to separate the pieces. Drop in mushrooms and boil everything for 2 more minutes. Stir in salt, pepper, chili pepper oil, and sesame oil. Serves 6.

PEKING AND NORTHERN CHINA

The gastronomic boundary of Northern China is not easy to demarcate with a specific style of food. This region covers a broad range of specialties of different provinces, religions, and nationalities which have all been classified as northern cooking because they happen to be located in a geographically homogeneous area of the North. But northern cooking could be seen as a composite of regional and culture variants such as imperial court, Mongolian, Moslem, Shantung, and Hopei dishes. Peking for centuries has been the capital, under several dynasties, and the center of cultural, political, economic, and intellectual activity. Its cuisine has fluctuated according to the rise and fall of different dynasties and their rulers, both Chinese and foreign. These constant changes have left Peking cooking a melting pot of foods and flavors. Hence, in terms of the cookery of Northern China, Peking is the perfect spot for representing the entire region.

In the Ming dynasty (1368-1644), great chefs from Shantung Province were hired to prepare food in the imperial palace. Many sophisticated dishes that characterize the cooking of Peking and the North today evolved from court dishes which originally came from Shantung. Shantung Province is noted for its light and refined cookery which uses chicken broth as a base. The liberal use of garlic, leeks, and onions in northern dishes is also an influence of Shantung. Many people of South China associate the northerners with garlic and strong-smelling breath. They may have their point, because northerners consume a great amount of garlicky herbs raw.

Poultry and seafood were favorite ingredients for the elegant court dishes and the haute cuisine of the upper classes. Even today, when chicken is plentiful and cheap, the Chinese consider it a festive food; it is almost the same attitude that Americans have toward turkeys. Though we can eat turkey all year round now, it still is the most important item on a Thanksgiving dinner table. Many exquisite dishes in this chapter such as Velvet Chicken, Chicken with Bean Curd, and Chicken Stir-Fried with Shrimp were all dishes from the palace.

During the time that China was under the reign of the Mongols (1280-1368) and Manchus (1644-1911), mutton and lamb were introduced into the country. Today, lamb and mutton dishes have become another characteristic of northern cuisine. There are a number of celebrated restaurants in Peking specializing in a wide range of scrumptious lamb dishes. Moslem-style broiled lamb shish kebab, Mongolian lamb hot pot and barbecued mutton, and Manchurian braised fragrant mutton are a few renowned lamb dishes of the North.

Northen China is a wheat-growing area, and flour, made into various forms of noodles, breads, and buns, serves as staple food. "Mandarin tortillas," pieces of thin bread shaped like Mexican tortillas, are used for wrapping up cooked food and eating it with the hands. These thin pancake-like breads are a must for eating Peking duck. They are also excellent served in lieu of rice with dishes such as Chicken with Green Peppers, Stir-Fried Peking Duck Meat with Bean Sprouts, and Stir-Fried Chicken with Bean Sprouts.

PEKING DUCK

Peking duck always turns a simple meal into a celebration. This renowned classic dish with its aromatic golden crackling skin and rich succulent meat deserves an ovation.

Traditionally, one Peking duck is eaten in four different ways. The first course, and the basic one, common to all Peking duck meals, is the crispy skin and the breast meat. It is eaten by cutting the meat and skin into bite-sized pieces, two or three morsels are placed on a piece of thin bread—in this book, this bread is called a Mandarin tortilla—along with some hoisin sauce and a small section of scallion or a cucumber stick; then the whole thing is rolled up like an egg roll and eaten with the hands. The remaining dishes are optional additions to this basic form of Peking duck. For the second course, the dark meat is stir-fried with bean sprouts or cabbage. In the third course, the bones and the carcass are boiled with vegetables and made into a soup; number four is a less popular egg custard dish. The drippings and fat from the duck are mixed with eggs and baked in a custard. Recipes for all four dishes are given in this book.

Preparation of Peking duck should be started two days prior to the day that it is going to be eaten. Put the duck in the oven two hours before serving time and serve it immediately after roasting.

> 1   duck, 5 lbs
> 10 cups water
> 1   Tbsp Shao-sing wine, sake, or dry sherry
> ¼   tsp salt
> 2   Tbsps maltose syrup or light corn syrup, or 1 Tbsp honey
> 1   Tbsp vinegar

Sauce

> ⅓   cup hoisin sauce
> 2   Tbsps water
> 1   Tbsp soy sauce
> ½   Tbsp sesame oil

Condiments

> 16 large scallions
> 1   large cucumber
> Mandarin tortillas (see page 143)

To make the duck:
Defrost the duck and wash under cold water. In a large pan, bring water to a boil. Turn off heat and put duck into the water; soak for 3 minutes. Remove duck from water and dry thoroughly inside and out with paper towels.

Rub duck cavity with wine and salt. In a small pan melt syrup and vinegar over a low fire, then rub mixture evenly over outside of duck. Tie a piece of strong cord around the neck of the duck. Hang duck in an airy place for at least 24 hours, until the skin is very dry. (Use chopsticks to keep wings and legs spread for maximum drying.)

Preheat oven to 325°. Set a rack on top of a roasting pan and place duck breast-side up on the rack. Roast duck in the lower part of the oven for 1½ to 2 hours, turning twice during roasting period. Drippings and fat will accumulate in the pan and the duck cavity; empty it while the duck is being turned over. Reserve the drippings and fat for Steamed Peking Duck Oil Custard, if desired.

Remove duck to a large plate or carving board. Cut the crisp skin from the duck into 1½-inch by 3-inch pieces and arrange, crisp side up, on a plate. When the skin is completely removed, cut the meat into the same size pieces, ¼ inch thick. Arrange on a plate. Serves 6 to 8.

To make the sauce:
While the duck is in the oven, in a small saucepan combine hoisin sauce, water, soy sauce, and sesame seed oil. Simmer for 2 minutes and pour into a bowl to cool.

To make scallion brushes:
While the duck is in the oven, remove roots and trim off most of the green leaves of the scallions and cut them into 3-inch pieces. Slit both ends lengthwise with a sharp knife, making a few intersecting cuts about ½ inch deep. Dip scallions in ice water and refrigerate until ready to use. Arrange them on a plate for serving.

To make cucumber sticks:
While the duck is in the oven, peel cucumber skin and cut off tip at both ends. Cut cucumber crosswise into 3-inch sections. Remove seeds and cut firm part into 1/3-inch square sticks. Arrange them neatly on a plate and refrigerate until ready to use.

薄
饼 Mandarin Tortillas

  2 cups all-purpose flour
  ¾ cup boiling water
  2 Tbsps oil

Put flour in a mixing bowl; make a well in the center, then pour in the boiling water. Mix flour and water to form a soft dough with a pair of chopsticks or a wooden spoon. Knead the hot dough for 5 minutes or until it is smooth. With a damp cloth or plastic wrapping, cover the dough and let it set for 30 minutes or longer.

Take dough out of bowl and knead for another minute or two on a lightly floured surface. Shape dough into a long sausage-like cylinder about 1½ inches in diameter and 14 inches in length. (For serving with Peking duck, shape dough into a cylinder 1 inch in diameter and 28 inches long.) Cut dough crosswise into 1-inch pieces, then flatten each piece with the palm of the hand into a round slice about 2 inches in diameter.

Brush one side of each slice with a thin layer of oil and then place 2 oiled sides against each other. Pair all the slices in that manner. With a rolling pin, roll each pair into thin pancakes about 6 to 7 inches in diameter (4 to 5 inches in diameter for those used with Peking duck).

Set a heavy skillet over a moderate flame. When the skillet is hot, toast the tortillas one pair at a time in an ungreased pan. As soon as a few brown spots appear on the bottom side, turn it over and toast the other side. Remove toasted tortillas from pan and separate each pair carefully. Stack tortillas on a plate and serve hot. If the tortillas are made ahead of time, they should be steamed for about 6 to 8 minutes before serving.

STIR-FRIED PEKING DUCK MEAT WITH BEAN SPROUTS

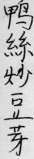

1 cup cooked Peking duck meat (remaining after
   serving Peking duck)
4 cups fresh bean sprouts
½ Tbsp Shao-sing wine or sake
1½ Tbsps light soy sauce
½ Tbsp cornstarch
¼ tsp sugar
   Dash white pepper
3 Tbsps oil
¼ cup coarsely chopped scallions
1 Tbsp finely shredded fresh chili peppers (optional)

Cut or tear the duck meat into slivers.

Rinse the bean sprouts and drain.

In a small bowl combine wine, soy sauce, cornstarch, sugar, and pepper. Set aside

Set a wok on high heat. When the pan is very hot, add 2 Tbsps oil and drop in the bean sprouts. Stir-fry bean sprouts constantly over high heat for 30 seconds; remove to a plate.

Heat the remaining 1 Tbsp of oil in a wok over high heat, stir in scallion and chili peppers, cook them in hot oil for 5 seconds; add duck meat, then the sauce mixture. When the sauce becomes slightly thickened, add bean sprouts. Toss and blend the meat and bean sprouts together. Transfer everything to a plate and serve. Serves 4.

北京鴨汤 PEKING DUCK SOUP

   1 duck carcass (remaining after serving Peking duck
        and stir-fried Peking duck meat)
   4 cups duck stock (boil the duck neck, liver, gizzard,
        and heart in 4 cups of water for 1 hour, strain, and
        discard neck and innards)
   2 slices of ginger
   1 scallion
  12 oz Chinese cabbage or bok choy
   1 cup soaked mung bean noodles (optional)
  ½ tsp salt (more or less according to taste)
   1 tsp sesame oil
      Dash black pepper

Put the bones in a saucepan, add stock, ginger and scallion.
Bring to a boil, then cover and simmer over moderate heat for ½
hour to 1 hour.

Rinse cabbage, or bok choy and cut into strips about ½ inch
wide.

Remove bones, ginger, and scallion from the soup. Add cabbage, or bok choy and mung bean noodles and cook for 10
minutes. Add salt, sesame oil, and black pepper. Transfer soup
to a serving bowl and serve hot. Serves 6 to 8.

STEAMED PEKING DUCK OIL CUSTARD

鴨
油
蒸
蛋

- 2 eggs, beaten
- ½ tsp salt
- 1 Tbsp light soy sauce
- 2 cups chicken stock, homemade (see page 23) or canned
- ½ cup Peking duck drippings and oil

In a bowl combine eggs with salt, soy sauce, and stock and mix well. Stir in duck drippings and oil; blend thoroughly. Pour egg mixture into a shallow bowl.

According to instructions on page 21, steam egg mixture over low heat for 20 minutes or until the custard is set. To obtain a smooth texture, avoid rapidly boiling water, and do not cover the pan tightly but leave a small crack open. Serves 6 to 8.

FRIED CHICKEN ROLLS

炸
鸡
卷

8 dried Chinese black mushrooms, about 1½ inches
   in diameter
8 oz boned chicken breast
½ Tbsp Shao-sing wine, sake, or dry sherry
½ tsp salt
½ cup shredded bamboo shoots or carrot
1 tsp sesame oil
3 egg whites, beaten
4 Tbsps flour
2 Tbsps cornstarch
½ cup Smithfield ham or baked ham, cut into thin
   slivers
½ cup shredded scallions
3 cups oil
   Szechuan peppercorn salt (see page 40)

Rinse mushrooms and soak in 1 cup of hot water for 30 minutes. Remove and discard stems, then cut the caps into thin slivers.

According to the instructions on page 16, cut chicken into 20 thin slices about 2 inches wide and 3½ inches long. Marinate chicken with wine and ¼ tsp salt.

Mix mushrooms and bamboo shoots or carrot with ⅛ tsp salt and the sesame oil.

Combine egg whites, flour, cornstarch, and the remaining one-quarter tsp salt. Mix thoroughly.

Brush a thin layer of the egg white mixture on one side of each piece of chicken. On top of the coated side, put a few strips of mushrooms and bamboo shoots or carrot, ham and scallions across the narrow end of each piece of chicken; roll chicken tightly and fasten with a toothpick.

Heat oil in a wok or a deep-fryer over high heat to 375°. Dip 5 or 6 chicken rolls into the batter and drop into hot oil. When the egg coating becomes firm, remove from oil and drain. Repeat with remaining chicken rolls. Reheat the oil till very hot, drop in half of the chicken rolls and fry until they become golden, remove and drain. Repeat with the other batch of chicken rolls. Serve at once with Szechuan peppercorn salt. Serves 4 to 6.

CHICKEN WITH BEAN CURD

鸡
球
豆
腐

    8   oz boned chicken, preferably dark meat
    2   Tbsps oil
    1   tsp minced garlic
    ½   tsp minced ginger
    ½   Tbsp Shao-sing wine, sake, or dry sherry
    1   cup chicken stock (see page 23)
    1   Tbsp soy sauce or oyster sauce
    ¼   tsp salt
    ¼   tsp sugar
    2   squares soft bean curd, 3 x 3 inches, cut up into 1-
          inch cubes
    1   Tbsp cornstarch dissolved in 2 Tbsps water
    1   Tbsp finely chopped scallion

Cut chicken into pieces ½ inch thick and 1 inch square.

Heat oil in a wok or a skillet over moderate heat. Stir in garlic and ginger, then add chicken. Cook and stir constantly for about 1 minute. Add wine, chicken stock, soy sauce or oyster sauce, salt, and sugar. Cover and simmer for 2 minutes. Uncover pan; add bean curd and cook for 1 minute until bean curd is thoroughly heated.

Stir in dissolved cornstarch and when sauce is thickened, transfer to a serving plate and garnish with chopped scallion. Serves 4.

CHICKEN WITH WALNUTS

合桃鸡丁

12   oz boned chicken breast
 1   Tbsp Shao-sing wine, sake, or dry sherry
 1   Tbsp cornstarch
 1   small egg white
 1   cup oil (see page 20 on stir-frying)
 ½   cup walnuts (or more)
 1   Tbsp hoisin sauce
 1   Tbsp soy sauce

Cut chicken meat into ⅔-inch by 1-inch cubes. In a large bowl mix chicken with wine, cornstarch, and egg white. Set aside.

Set wok over medium heat, pour in oil; when the oil is hot but not smoking, pour in walnuts and fry until light brown. With a slotted spoon or strainer, scoop out walnuts from oil and let cool on a piece of paper towel, leaving oil in wok.

Reheat oil in the wok over moderate heat; when oil is hot, put in chicken and fry for about 1 minute or until chicken becomes firm and white. Remove chicken and oil from wok and drain chicken in a strainer. Reserve the oil.

Place wok back on moderate heat, spoon 1 Tbsp reserved oil into wok, add hoisin sauce, cook the sauce for a few seconds to bring out the flavor, then quickly add cooked chicken and soy sauce, stir-fry rapidly, and mix sauce with chicken evenly (if the sauce is too dry, add 1 Tbsp water), then add walnuts and mix well. Remove chicken and walnuts to plate and serve at once. Serves 4.

VELVET CHICKEN

芙
蓉
鸡
片

This delectable, elegant dish can be prepared ahead of time and reheated. To retain the fresh green color of the green peas, they should be added to velvet chicken just before the dish is to be reheated.

   10 oz boned chicken breast
   ⅓ cup chicken stock (see page 23)
    1 Tbsp Shao-sing wine, sake, or dry sherry
   ½ tsp salt
        Dash white pepper
    2 tsps cornstarch
    4 egg whites
    2 cups oil
   ¼ cup fresh or frozen peas
   ½ Tbsp cornstarch dissolved in ⅔ cup of chicken stock
    1 Tbsp cooked Smithfield ham, minced

Puree chicken according to instructions on page 17.

In a bowl mix minced chicken meat with stock, wine, ¼ tsp salt, and the white pepper and cornstarch to make a thin paste, then blend in the egg whites. Do not beat the egg whites.

Set a wok on top of medium heat, pour in oil, and when the oil is just hot (do not overheat oil, chicken and egg white must not turn brown), scoop chicken puree into oil with a big spoon, or pour ¼ cup at a time into oil. As soon as chicken turns white and firm, remove from oil and drain. Empty all but 1 Tbsp oil from wok.

Set wok back on medium heat, add the remaining ¼ tsp salt, and stir in peas; stir-fry the peas for 30 seconds. Pour in the cornstarch and chicken stock mixture, stir until it thickens, then fold in the cooked chicken. Transfer velvet chicken to a plate and sprinkle minced ham on top. Serve at once. Serves 4.

DICED CHICKEN WITH SWEET BEAN PASTE

将
酱
爆
鸡
丁

12 oz boned chicken breast, diced
¼ tsp salt
1 Tbsp Shao-sing wine, sake, or dry sherry
1 Tbsp cornstarch
1 small egg white
1 Tbsp soy sauce
1 Tbsp sweet bean paste
2 Tbsps chicken stock or water (see page 23)
1 tsp sesame oil
1 cup oil (see page 20 on stir-frying)
½ Tbsp minced ginger
3 Tbsps chopped scallion
½ cup diced water chestnuts or bamboo shoots

Mix chicken with salt, ½ Tbsp wine, and the cornstarch and egg white.

In a small bowl combine soy sauce, sweet bean paste, chicken stock, sesame oil, and the remaining ½ Tbsp wine.

Heat oil in a wok over moderate heat until hot but not smoking. Drop in chicken, stir to separate the pieces, and cook until meat becomes white and firm, about 1 minute.

With a slotted spoon, remove chicken from oil and drain. Empty all but 1 Tbsp oil from wok, add ginger and scallion. Stir and cook for about 30 seconds. Add cooked chicken and water chestnuts or bamboo shoots, then stir in the soy sauce and bean paste mixture from the bowl. Mix everything thoroughly. Transfer to a plate and serve. This dish can be reheated in the microwave oven. Serves 4.

炸 **DEEP-FRIED CHICKEN**
鸡 **BALLS**
丸

Chicken balls can be prepared in advance and reheated in the oven or microwave oven. They are perfect served as an appetizer with commercial duck sauce (plum sauce).

    12 oz ground chicken meat
     2 Tbsps minced or ground pork fat (optional)
     1 Tbsp Shao-sing wine, sake, or dry sherry
    ¼ cup chopped scallions
     1 Tbsp soy sauce
    ⅛ tsp salt
    ¼ tsp sugar
     1 Tbsp cornstarch
     1 egg, separated
    ½ cup finely chopped water chestnuts
     2 cups oil

In a mixing bowl, combine chicken with pork, wine, scallions, soy sauce, salt, sugar, cornstarch, and egg yoke. Beat the mixture until it becomes elastic. Whip egg white until stiff and fold in with the chicken mixture, then add water chestnuts.

Heat oil in a wok or a deep-fryer over medium heat until oil is about 375° or almost smoking. With your hand and a teaspoon, scoop up marble-sized balls of chicken mixture and drop them into the oil. Deep-fry about 8 to 10 balls at a time until golden brown, about 2 minutes. Remove balls with a strainer and drain. Repeat until all the mixture is used. Serves 4 to 6.

STIR-FRIED CHICKEN WITH ZUCCHINI OR CUCUMBER

黄
瓜
炒
鸡
片

2 Tbsps dried tree ears (optional)
8 oz boned chicken breast
½ Tbsp Shao-sing wine, sake, or dry sherry
¼ tsp salt
½ Tbsp cornstarch
1 small egg white
1 Tbsp soy sauce
¼ tsp sugar
1 tsp sesame oil
½ cup oil (see page 20 on stir-frying)
2 cups sliced zucchinin or 1 cup cucumber
2 Tbsps chicken stock (see page 23) or water
1 tsp minced ginger
1 tsp cornstarch dissolved in 1 Tbsp water

Soak dried tree ears in 1 cup hot water for 30 minutes. Rinse thoroughly, remove sand and tough woody tips. Tear or cut large ones into smaller pieces.

According to instructions on page 16, cut chicken into thin slices about 1 inch by 2 inches. Mix chicken with wine, ⅛ tsp salt, and the cornstarch and egg white.

In a small bowl, combine soy sauce, sugar, and sesame oil.

Heat oil in a wok or a skillet over moderate heat until hot but not smoking. Drop in chicken, stir to separate the pieces; cook until meat becomes firm, about 1 minute. With a slotted spoon, remove meat from oil and drain. Empty all but 1 Tbsp oil from pan and reserve the rest; set over high heat, add tree ears, zucchini or cucumber, and the remaining salt. Stir for 30 seconds, add 2 Tbsps chicken stock or water; cover and cook for 1 minute. Transfer to a plate. Heat 1 Tbsp reserved oil in the pan, stir in ginger and cook for 5 seconds, then drop in chicken and add the soy sauce mixture. Blend in the zucchini or cucumber and tree ears, then thicken with the dissolved cornstarch. Transfer to a plate and serve. Serves 4.

三杯鸡腿 BRAISED ONE-TWO-THREE DRUMSTICKS

This is "as easy as one, two, three," and is excellent when served cold for buffets or picnics. The dish is christened by me; its Chinese name is "Three-Cup Chicken," representing 1 cup soy sauce, I cup wine, and 1 cup sesame oil. However, when following the three-cup principle the finished dish is very salty and oily. In order to make the dish more pleasing to American tastes, I have come up with the following version.

> 8 chicken drumsticks
> ¼ cup Shao-sing wine or sake (no other substitute)
> ½ cup soy sauce
> ¼ cup sesame oil
> ½ Tbsp sugar
> ½ cup chicken stock (see page 23) or water
> 3 scallions, cut into 3-inch sections
> 3 slices of ginger, 1 inch in diameter

Place all the ingredients in a saucepan that is just big enough for all the drumsticks to be arranged in one layer. Bring to a boil over high heat, then reduce heat; cover pan and simmer for 30 minutes. Serve hot or cold. Serves 4.

STIR-FRIED CHICKEN OR TURKEY WITH LEEKS

青蒜炒鸡丝

  8 oz boneless chicken or turkey breast
  ½ Tbsp Shao-sing wine, sake, or dry sherry
  ¼ tsp salt
  ½ Tbsp cornstarch
  1 small egg white
  1 Tbsp soy sauce
  ¼ tsp sugar
  1 tsp sesame oil
  1 Tbsp water
  ½ cup oil (see page 20 on stir-frying)
  3 cups leeks, cut into thin strips about 2 inches long
  1 tsp minced garlic

Cut chicken or turkey into thin slivers according to instructions on page 16. Mix chicken with wine, ⅛ tsp salt, cornstarch, and egg white.

In a small bowl, combine soy sauce, sugar, sesame oil, and 1 Tbsp water.

Heat oil in a wok or a skillet over moderate heat until hot but not smoking. Drop in chicken or turkey, stir to separate the strips; cook until meat becomes firm, about 1 minute. With a slotted spoon, remove meat from oil and drain. Empty all but 2 Tbsps oil from pan, set over high heat, add leeks, garlic, and the remaining ⅛ tsp salt. Stir and cook until leeks become soft. Add cooked chicken and soy sauce mixture and blend thoroughly. Transfer to a plate and serve. Serves 4.

MU SHU CHICKEN

木
须
鸡
肉

During my many years of teaching Chinese cooking, I have met many students who do not eat pork. Instead of depriving them of those delicious classic pork dishes, I learned to substitute chicken for pork. In this book you will find a great number of recipes which are the chicken versions of pork dishes. This dish is a superb example.

This dish is usually eaten wrapped with a thin crepelike flour bread—in this book called Mandarin tortillas. Half a teaspoonful of sweet sauce is spread on a tortilla, then 2 or 3 tablespoonsful of Mu Shu Chicken are placed in the middle of it. The whole thing is then rolled up like an enchilada or egg roll and eaten with the hands. It makes a perfect one-dish meal. The sweet sauce is optional; I like mine without.

For people who like pork, simply substitute the same amount of lean pork for the chicken in this recipe.

> 3 Tbsps dried tree ears
> ½ cup soaked tiger lily buds or bamboo shoots, shredded
> 12 oz boned chicken breast
> ½ Tbsp Shao-sing wine, sake, or dry sherry
> 2 Tbsps soy sauce
> ¼ tsp sugar
> ½ Tbsp cornstarch
> ½ cup oil (see page 20 on stir-frying)
> 3 eggs, beaten
> 2 cups shredded savoy cabbage, firmly packed
> 1 cup shredded scallions, firmly packed
> ½ cup chicken stock (see page 23)
> 1 recipe Mandarin tortillas (see page 143)
> Sweet sauce (see page 157)

Soak dried tree ears in 2 cups hot water for 30 minutes. Rinse thoroughly, remove sand and tough woody tips. Tear large ones into small pieces.

Cut off tough stem ends from tiger lily buds, then cut each bud in half crosswise.

According to instructions on page 16, cut chicken into thin strips. Mix chicken with wine, 1 Tbsp soy sauce, and the sugar and cornstarch.

Heat ½ Tbsp oil in a wok or skillet over moderate heat, pour in eggs; swirl around and cook till the eggs are set. Transfer eggs to plate and cut them up into small pieces.

Heat the remaining oil in the same pan until hot but not smoking; add chicken and stir to separate the pieces. Cook for about 40 seconds; remove chicken from oil and drain. Empty all but 1 Tbsp oil from pan, drop in cabbage, and stir-fry for 1 minute. Add scallion, stir and cook with the cabbage for 30 seconds. Mix in tree ears, tiger lily buds or bamboo shoots, the remaining 1 Tbsp soy sauce, and the chicken stock. Cover and cook over high heat for 1 minute, uncover, blend in the cooked chicken. Transfer the whole contents to a plate and serve with Mandarin tortillas and sweet sauce (if desired). Serves 4 to 6.

 ## Sweet Sauce for Mu Shu Chicken

¼ cup hoisin sauce
1 Tbsp soy sauce
2 Tbsps water
1 tsp sesame oil

In a small saucepan combine hoisin sauce with soy sauce and water and bring to a boil over low heat. Simmer for 2 minutes, then stir in sesame oil. Transfer to a bowl and cool.

STIR-FRIED CHICKEN WITH BEAN SPROUTS

芽
菜
炒
鸡
絲

6 oz boned chicken or turkey breast
¼ tsp salt
½ Tbsp Shao-sing wine, sake, or dry sherry
½ egg white
1 Tbsp cornstarch
1½ Tbsps soy sauce
½ tsp sugar
Dash white pepper
1 tsp sesame oil
2 Tbsps chicken stock (see page 23) or water
5 cups fresh bean sprouts, about 2 inches long
½ cup oil (see page 20 on stir-frying)
1 tsp minced ginger
½ cup chopped scallions

Cut chicken into very thin strips about 2 inches long and ⅛ inch around, according to instructions on page 16. Mix chicken with salt, wine, egg white, and ½ Tbsp cornstarch.

In a small bowl combine soy sauce, sugar, pepper, the remaining ½ Tbsp cornstarch, and the sesame oil and chicken stock or water.

Rinse the bean sprouts and drain well.

Heat oil in a wok over moderate heat; add the chicken and stir to separate the pieces. Cook for 1 minute, then with a slotted spoon, remove chicken and drain. Empty all but 2 Tbsps oil from wok; add ginger and scallions, stir them in hot oil for 20 seconds. Drop in bean sprouts and toss them constantly over high heat for 30 seconds, then add chicken and the soy sauce mixture from the bowl. Toss and blend thoroughly. When the sauce is thickened, transfer the entire contents to a plate and serve at once. Serves 3.

STIR-FRIED CHICKEN OR DUCK HEARTS WITH SCALLIONS

During my childhood days, my craving was not for sweets but rather for delicacies such as duck gizzards and chicken hearts. Today, they are still my great favorites. I feel very privileged to be living in America where I am able to buy chicken hearts and gizzards by the pound and do not have to practice my fast draw with the chopsticks to reach for the only chicken heart on the table.

10 oz chicken or duck hearts
½ Tbsp cornstarch
1 Tbsp Shao-sing wine, sake, or dry sherry
12 good-sized scallions
1 Tbsp soy sauce
¼ tsp sugar
½ Tbsp vinegar
   Dash white pepper
1 tsp sesame oil
¼ tsp salt
½ cup oil (see page 20 for stir-frying)

Remove fat from hearts, score the larger ones by making 4 lengthwise cuts on each of them, then cut each one in two lengthwise. Mix hearts with cornstarch and ½ Tbsp wine.

Rinse scallions, split each stalk lengthwise to separate the layers, then cut into 1-inch lengths.

In a small bowl, combine soy sauce, sugar, vinegar, pepper, sesame oil, ¼ tsp salt, and the remaining ½ Tbsp wine.

Heat oil in wok over moderate heat until hot. Add hearts and stir to separate the pieces. Cook for 2 minutes. With a slotted spoon, remove hearts from oil and drain.

Empty all but 2 Tbsps oil from wok, heat over high heat, drop in scallions. Toss and cook for 1 minute or until scallions become soft. Add cooked hearts and the mixture from the bowl; blend thoroughly. Transfer to a plate and serve. Serves 2 to 4.

熏鸡 SMOKED CHICKEN

Smoking is a common Chinese method of preserving meat. Nowadays although meat is smoked with wood chips for the commercial market, Chinese people usually smoked their meat, fish, or poultry at home with a mixture of tea leaves, brown sugar, and rice. Sometimes spices are added to the mixture to provide a richer flavor. See smoked turkey (page 19).

> 1 chicken, 3 lbs
> 3 Tbsps salt
> ½ Tbsp sugar
> 3 scallions, crushed and cut into 2-inch sections
> 5 slices of fresh ginger, about 1 inch in diameter, crushed
> ½ tsp Szechuan peppercorns
> ⅓ cup soy sauce
> ½ cup brown sugar
> ½ cup rice
> 1 Tbsp black tea leaves (optional)

Wash chicken in cold water and dry inside and out with paper towels.

Combine salt, sugar, scallions, and ginger.

Rub chicken inside and out with the salt mixture, then cover in a bowl and refrigerate overnight.

Put chicken in a saucepan just big enough to hold it; add Szechuan peppercorns, soy sauce, and enough boiling water to cover ¾ of the chicken. Cover pan and bring to a boil over high heat, then reduce the heat to low and cook for 20 minutes. Remove chicken from liquid promptly and cool.

According to instructions on page 19, smoke chicken with brown sugar, rice, and tea leaves for 10 minutes over medium heat.

Remove chicken and chop into 1-inch by 2-inch pieces according to instructions on page 13. Arrange neatly on a serving plate. Serve chicken warm or at room temperature. Serves 6 to 8.

CHICKEN STIR-FRIED WITH SHRIMP

鸡
丁
虾
仁

8 oz boned chicken breast
1 Tbsp Shao-sing wine, sake, or dry sherry
⅛ tsp salt
1½ Tbsps cornstarch
1 large egg white
8 oz medium-sized shrimp, each one shelled and split in half
3 Tbsps chicken stock (see page 23)
1½ Tbsps soy sauce
¼ tsp sugar
1 tsp sesame oil
Dash black or white pepper
½ cup oil (see page 20 on stir-frying)
1 tsp minced garlic
1 tsp minced ginger
½ cup diced water chestnuts
¼ cup fresh or defrosted-frozen peas

Dice chicken into ½ inch squares. Mix chicken with ½ Tbsp wine, the salt, ½ Tbsp cornstarch, and ½ the egg white.

In separate bowl mix shrimp with the remaining ½ Tbsp wine, ½ Tbsp cornstarch, and the remaining ½ egg white.

In another small bowl combine chicken stock, soy sauce, sugar, sesame oil, pepper, and the remaining ½ Tbsp cornstarch.

Heat oil in a wok or skillet over moderate heat until hot but not smoking; add chicken, stirring to separate the pieces. Cook for 1 minute or until chicken becomes white and firm. With a slotted spoon, remove chicken from oil and drain. Add shrimp to the remaining oil in the pan; stir and separate them. Cook for 40 seconds. Remove shrimp from oil with a slotted spoon and drain.

Empty all but 1 Tbsp oil from pan, drop in garlic and ginger and stir in hot oil for 15 seconds. Add chicken, shrimp, water chestnuts, and the sauce from the small bowl; blend everything thoroughly and mix in peas. Transfer to a plate and serve. Serves 4.

BRAISED CHICKEN GIZZARDS

> 1 lb chicken gizzards
> 7½ cups water
> 4 scallions, cut into 3-inch sections
> 2 slices of ginger, about 1 inch in diameter
> 1 whole star anise or 8 small sections
> 3 Tbsps Shao-sing wine or sake (no other substitute)
> ¼ cup soy sauce
> 1 Tbsp sugar

Remove fat from gizzards; check the inside of each one and remove yellow lining if any. In a saucepan bring 6 cups of water to a boil; blanch gizzards for 1 minute or until the outside layer becomes white. Drain and rinse thoroughly with cold water.

In a heavy pan, combine gizzards with scallions, ginger, star anise, wine, soy sauce, sugar, and the remaining 1½ cups water. Bring to a boil over high heat, then cover and simmer over low heat for 2 hours. At the end of the cooking, if there is still a lot of liquid left, turn the heat up and let boil until it reduces to only ⅓ cup. Before serving, slice each gizzard into pieces ¼ inch thick, place them on a plate, and pour sauce over. Serve hot or cold. Serves 4 to 6.

SWEET AND SOUR CHICKEN

甜
酸
鸡

1 lb chicken meat, either white or dark
1 Tbsp Shao-sing wine, sake, or dry sherry
2 Tbsps soy sauce
4 Tbsps lemon juice
　 Dash white pepper
5 Tbsps cornstarch
1 Tbsp sugar
¾ cup pineapple juice
1 tsp sesame oil
1 cup oil
1 large green pepper, with seeds removed and cut
　　 into 1-inch squares
1 tsp minced ginger
1 tsp minced garlic
4 slices canned pineapple, cut into 1-inch lengths

Cut chicken into ¾-inch cubes and mix with wine, 1 Tbsp soy sauce, 1 Tbsp lemon juice, the pepper, and 4 Tbsps cornstarch.

In a small bowl mix together the remaining 1 Tbsp soy sauce, 3 Tbsps lemon juice, and 1 Tbsp cornstarch with the sugar, pineapple juice, and sesame oil.

Heat oil in a wok until hot about 370°, drop in half of the chicken one piece at a time and deep-fry over moderate heat for 2 minutes. Remove with a strainer and drain. Cook the remaining chicken cubes in the same way and drain. After the chicken has been fried, drop green pepper into the oil and deep-fry for 30 seconds. Remove from oil with a slotted spoon or a strainer, and drain.

Empty all but 1 Tbsp oil from wok. Add ginger and garlic to oil and cook for 15 seconds over moderate heat. Pour in sweet-and-sour sauce from bowl and bring to a boil. Heat and stir until sauce is thickened. Add green pepper, pineapple, and fried chicken; blend thoroughly. Transfer to a plate and serve at once. Serves 4.

Note: The sauce and the frying can be done in advance. Just before serving, reheat the oil till very hot and fry the chicken again for 1 minute. Heat up the sauce in a saucepan or in the microwave oven and combine with the chicken.

CORNISH GAME HEN SHANGTUNG STYLE

1 Cornish game hen
4 Tbsps soy sauce
1 tsp sugar
½ cup oil
½ tsp salt
6 slices of ginger, about 1 inch in diameter
6 scallions, cut into 2-inch sections
2 tsps Szechuan peppercorns
½ Tbsp vinegar
1 tsp sesame oil

Rinse Cornish game hen; drain well. Dry inside and out with paper towels. Soak hen in 3 Tbsps soy sauce mixed with the sugar for 3 hours, turning the hen a few times to allow an even coating of soy sauce.

Heat oil in a wok and brown hen in oil over high heat until the skin becomes dark brown. Place hen in a shallow bowl; rub the cavity with ¼ tsp salt and insert 2 slices of ginger, 2 scallions, and 1 tsp Szechuan peppercorns into it. Sprinkle the rest of the salt on the outside and place the remaining ginger, scallions, and peppercorns on top of the bird. Cover and steam for 45 minutes according to the instructions on page 21.

In a small bowl combine the remaining 1 Tbsp soy sauce with the vinegar and sesame oil.

Remove Cornish game hen from pan. With two forks, pull and tear the meat into bite-sized strips (leaving the carcass and the bones on the plate). Serve with the soy sauce and vinegar mixture. This dish can be prepared in advance and reheated. Serves 2 to 4.

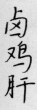

BRAISED CHICKEN LIVERS

    12 oz chicken livers
     6 cups water
     4 scallions, cut into 3-inch sections
     2 slices of ginger, about 1 inch in diameter
     1 whole star anise or 8 small sections
     2 Tbsps Shao-sing wine or sake (no other substitute)
     3 Tbsps soy sauce
    ½ Tbsp sugar
     1 tsp sesame oil

In a saucepan bring 5 cups of water to a boil, blanch livers for 1 minute, and drain. In a pot combine livers with scallions, ginger, anise, wine, soy sauce, sugar, and the remaining 1 cup water. Bring to a boil over high heat; cover and simmer over low heat for 30 minutes. After 30 minutes, if there is still a lot of liquid in the pan, turn the heat up and let boil until only about ⅓ cup liquid is left.

Slice liver into ½-inch pieces, place on a serving plate, pour the sauce over, and sprinkle with sesame oil. Serve hot or cold. Serves 4 to 6.

STIR-FRIED CHICKEN WITH GREEN PEPPERS

青椒炒鸡絲

Pair this dish with Mu Shu Chicken (page 156) or Chicken Stir-Fried with Bean Sprouts (page 158), serve with Mandarin tortillas, and enjoy a typical Northern Chinese dinner. Every diner wraps his or her own roll of supper. A very attractive way to entertain friends.

10 oz boned chicken breast
½ Tbsp Shao-sing wine, sake, or dry sherry
¼ tsp salt
     Dash white pepper
 2 tsps cornstarch
½ egg white
 3 medium-sized green peppers
½ cup oil (see page 20 on stir-frying)
 1 Tbsp light soy sauce

Cut chicken into very fine strips, about 2 inches, according to instructions on page 16. In a bowl mix chicken with wine, salt, pepper, cornstarch, and egg white. Set aside.

Wash green peppers, then cut in two lengthwise. Remove seeds and cut the peppers into ⅛-inch-wide strips.

Heat oil in a wok over moderate heat; when oil is hot but not smoking, add chicken. Stir and separate the strips; cook for about 1 minute or until chicken becomes white and firm. Remove chicken from oil and drain. Empty all but 1 Tbsp oil from wok; heat the remaining oil over moderate heat. Add green peppers and stir-fry for 2 minutes. Peppers should be tender but still green and crunchy. Add chicken and light soy sauce, blend everything together thoroughly. Transfer to a plate and serve at once. Serves 4.

CHICKEN AND BEAN SPROUT SALAD

冷拌豆芽鸡絲

1 chicken breast with rib bones, about 12 oz
8 cups water
3 cups fresh bean sprouts
1 large cucumber
½ Tbsp sesame seeds
3 Tbsps soy sauce
2 Tbsps vinegar
½ tsp sugar
1 Tbsp prepared mustard (optional)
1 Tbsp sesame oil

Steam chicken breast in a steamer or on top of a rack in a saucepan filled with water to an inch below the rack. Bring water to a rapid boil, cover pan, and steam for 20 minutes. Remove chicken from steamer and chill.

In a saucepan bring 8 cups of water to a boil over moderate heat; drop in bean sprouts. Stir the bean sprouts in hot water for about 5 seconds, then drain off hot water quickly and rinse with cold water until bean sprouts are cool. Drain bean sprouts in a colander and set aside.

Peel cucumber and cut it crosswise into 2½-inch sections. Cut the outer part of the sections into thin slices and discard the seeds. Shred the thin slices into slivers.

Toast sesame seeds in an ungreased cast-iron skillet over low heat until golden brown. Transfer to a plate and cool.

Mix cucumber and bean sprouts together, then put them on a serving plate.

Bone chicken and tear the meat into slivers by hand. Arrange chicken on top of the vegetables and garnish with toasted sesame seeds.

In a bowl mix soy sauce, vinegar, sugar, mustard, and sesame oil together. Pour sauce over chicken and vegetables just before serving. Mix everything together at the table in front of the diners. Serves 4 to 6.

鸡冻 JELLIED CHICKEN

The traditional method of preparing Jellied Chicken is to cook the chicken with pork skin for a long time until the sauce becomes gelatinous. This recipe depends on the chicken juices to form the aspic.

> 2 chicken breasts with rib bones, about 1 lb each
> 1½ Tbsps Shao-sing wine, sake, or dry sherry
> ⅛ tsp salt
> Dash black pepper
> 6 slices of ginger root, about 1½ inches in diameter
> 2 scallions, cut into 2-inch sections
> ¼ cup soy sauce
> 1 tsp sugar
> 1 Tbsp sesame oil
> 3 to 4 small sprigs of parsley

Wash chicken and dry with paper towel. Rub chicken with ½ Tbsp wine, salt, and pepper. Place chicken breasts side by side in a big bowl and spread ginger slices and scallions over them.

Fill a big saucepan or a wok with about 1½ to 2 inches of water, then place a rack or a ring in the middle of the pan and set the bowl of chicken on top of the rack. Cover pan and steam for 30 minutes over moderate heat. Remove chicken from bowl and cool. Reserve the stock in the bowl.

In a small pan combine the remaining wine, soy sauce, sugar, sesame oil, and the reserved chicken stock and bring the mixture to a boil over medium heat. Add chicken and boil for 30 seconds on each side. Remove from heat and cool. When it is cold enough to handle with bare hands, bone the chicken according to instructions on page 14, soak the meat in the cooking liquid, and chill.

Cut chicken and the aspic into serving pieces, according to the instructions on page 13. Garnish with parsley and serve cold. Serves 6.

SWEET AND SOUR CHICKEN GIZZARDS WITH PINEAPPLE

菠
萝
腎
月
球

     8 chicken gizzards
     1 Tbsp salt
     1 tsp minced ginger
     1 Tbsp Shao-sing wine, sake, or dry sherry
  1½ Tbsps cornstarch
     2 Tbsps catsup
     2 Tbsps vinegar
     1 Tbsp sugar
    ½ cup pineapple juice
    ½ Tbsp soy sauce
     1 cup oil
     2 medium-sized green peppers, or one green and one
          red, seeded and diced
     1 tsp minced garlic
     3 Tbsps chopped scallion
     4 slices of canned pineapple rings, each one cut into
          5 small chunks

Peel off yellow inside lining of chicken gizzards if any; remove the fat on the outside. Rub gizzards with 1 Tbsp salt, then rinse thoroughly and drain.

Cut each gizzard into four pieces by separating first the two cuplike pieces, then cut each half crosswise into two pieces. For even cooking, score each piece with 3 to 4 cuts about ½ inch deep. Mix chicken gizzards with ginger, wine, and 1 Tbsp cornstarch.

In a small bowl combine catsup, vinegar, sugar, pineapple juice, soy sauce, and the remaining ½ Tbsp cornstarch.

Heat oil in a wok over high heat; when oil is hot, almost smoking, drop in gizzards, stir to separate the pieces, and fry for 30 seconds. Quickly remove gizzards from oil with a strainer and drain. Empty all but 1 Tbsp oil, set over high heat, add peppers, garlic, and scallion, and stir-fry everything for 30 seconds. Return gizzards to pan and cook with the peppers for 20 more seconds. Pour in sweet and sour sauce, add pineapple; stir continuously until sauce is thickened. Transfer to a plate and serve at once. Serves 4.

SMOKED TURKEY

Smoked turkey, of course, is an adaptation of smoked chicken. It is delicious, plentiful, and economical, a perfect dish to have for large gatherings on any occasion. Although it takes some ingenuity and five days to complete the whole process, it actually does not require constant attention. The reward is greater than the effort put into the dish.

After smoking, the turkey can be stored in the refrigerator for as long as 10 days. Slice the meat into paper-thin pieces before serving.

    1 turkey, 10 to 12 lbs
    8 Tbsps salt
    2 Tbsps sugar
    ½ cup Shao-sing wine, sake, or dry sherry
    6 Tbsps Szechuan peppercorns
   10 scallions, crushed and cut into 2-inch sections
   14 slices of ginger, about 1 inch in diameter, crushed
    2 whole star anise or 16 small sections, crushed into
         small broken pieces with mortar and pestle
    1 Tbsp fennel seeds
    4 sticks cinnamon, crushed into small broken pieces
         with mortar and pestle
    1 Tbsp black tea leaves
    ½ cup raw rice
    ½ cup brown sugar

Rinse turkey thoroughly and rub inside and out with paper towels.

In a bowl mix salt, sugar, wine, 4 Tbsps Szechuan peppercorns, and the scallion sections and ginger slices. Rub turkey inside and out with the mixture, insert ⅓ of the mixture inside the cavity, and coat the rest all over the turkey. Put turkey in a large salad bowl and cover with a big plastic bag. Cover and store in the refrigerator for 3 days; turn turkey over a couple of times a day.

Remove and discard ginger, scallions and Szechuan peppercorns from the turkey. Put a poultry roasting rack in a pot or a covered roasting pan large enough to accommodate the turkey. Fill the bottom of the pan with 3 inches of boiling water. Adjust the roasting rack and place the turkey on it, breast-side up. The water level should be barely touching the back of the bird. Cover tightly and steam over moderate heat for 1 hour and 15 minutes. Do not overcook the turkey. Check the water level after 45 minutes; if much water has evaporated, replenish with boiling water, immediately cover the pan and turn the heat to high for 5 minutes, then finish steaming with moderate heat. Lift turkey from pan and place it in a colander with the tail opening facing down; drain and cool the bird for 6 hours or longer.

Smoke turkey according to instructions on page 19. Mix the remaining 2 Tbsps Szechuan peppercorns with the crushed star anise, fennel seeds, crushed cinnamon sticks, and black tea. Spread the spices on the bottom of the pan, then the rice over the spices, and lastly sprinkle brown sugar over the rice. Cover and smoke over a moderate heat for 15 minutes.

After smoking, chill the turkey in the refrigerator overnight. Slice the meat paper-thin and serve. Serves about 20.

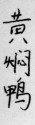

BRAISED DUCK WITH GARLIC

   1 *duck, about 4 lbs*
   2 *Tbsps oil*
   3 *slices of ginger, about 1 inch in diameter*
 10 *large cloves of garlic, peeled and sliced into thin*
      pieces
   1 *cup bamboo shoots, cut into chunks*
 ¼ *cup Shao-sing wine or sake (no other substitute)*
   2 *Tbsps soy sauce*
   1 *tsp sugar*
   1 *tsp salt*
   2 *cups chicken stock (see page 23)*
   1 *Tbsp cornstarch dissolved in 3 Tbsps water*
      Dash black pepper
   1 *tsp sesame oil*

Rinse duck and drain. Remove fat, duck tail, and the skin. Cut duck into chunks according to instructions on page 13 on how to cut raw poultry into serving pieces.

In a large pot, bring 8 cups of water to a boil and drop in duck pieces. Blanch for 2 to 3 minutes and drain.

Heat oil in a heavy pan over moderate heat; add ginger and garlic and cook for 30 seconds. Add duck, bamboo shoots, wine, soy sauce, sugar, salt, and stock; cover and simmer over low heat for 1 hour. At the end of the hour, uncover pan and boil over high heat until only about ⅔ of juices remain in the pan. Thicken sauce with dissolved cornstarch and sprinkle pepper and sesame oil over duck. Transfer to a plate and serve. This dish can be prepared in advance and reheated. Serves 4 to 6.

SHANGHAI AND EAST-CENTRAL CHINA

The Chinese call this region "Land of Fish and Rice," which is certainly very appropriate, because the land around the Yangtze River basin is most fertile for rice planting and is covered with countless lakes and rivers that abound with infinite varieties of fish. Along this stretch of rich land stand some of the most important cities of China: Shanghai, Nanking, Soochow, Hang-chow, and Wuhan. This region is blessed the year around with both natural bounty and rich cultivated resources. Because it is located along the banks of China's most important waterway and is the center of the nation's commerce and industry, the lower Yangtze region has developed a culinary art that is one of the best known in China. The cooking of this area perhaps does not have the glamorous historical background of northern food, nor the elegant and exquisite style of southern dishes, but it is a distinctive cuisine of great sophistication.

Records show that many of the local dishes were highly admired by Chinese emperors. In the old days, during the hot summer months, emperors and officials would travel to Hang-chow and Soochow on vacation. The royal families liked the regional food so much that upon their return to Peking, they ordered that the same dishes be produced in the imperial kitchens. Eventually a great number of southern specialties were added to the imperial court menus and received the high esteem that enabled them to challenge the best foods of the North.

Apart from marinating poultry and seafood in wine, the unique local method of preparing food, the culinary practices of the East-Central region are more or less the same as in other places: steaming, stir-frying, smoking, and braising. Of all these methods, perhaps braising meat with vegetables and soy sauce can be said to be the most typical style of this area. Chicken and ducks are often simmered with tasty pickled vegetables in stock and soy sauce. The finished dish is a rich and mellow exchange of flavors. Soy sauce and sugar are two of the favorite seasoning agents used in dishes of this region, thus many of the dishes are dark in color and robust in taste. Famous throughout China are the elaborate and intricately prepared poultry dishes, the most impressive of which are chicken stuffed in a watermelon and steamed (page 214); boned duck stuffed with sweet rice and nuts, then braised with soy sauce; and morsels of chicken meat wrapped with cellophane paper and deep-fried (page 182). In addition to these delights, there are the renowned Nanking Cold Salted Duck (page 197), Soochow Soy Sauce Duck (page 200), Drunken Chicken of Shanghai (page 181), and Beggar's Chicken of Jiangsu Province (page 179), which is wrapped in lotus leaves and coated with mud, then baked for 5 to 6 hours.

There are other regional specialties such as the hors d'oeuvres which are cooked and served cold. Shanghai and Nanking are particularly famous for these dainties. At an elegant banquet the prepared cold foods are served at the beginning of the meal as appetizers, while in restaurants these dishes are displayed on the counter in front of the shop and the diners can make a choice of which dishes to go with the rice. But the greatest culinary pride of this area is centered on their desserts, sweet dumplings made of glutinous rice powder and stuffed with rich sweet fillings, then formed into dazzling shapes of birds, goldfish, flowers, and fruit of all kinds.

Because rice is abundant here this is also wine-producing country, for the rice is used to make both vinegar and wine. The Shao-sing wine we use for cooking in this book is a noted product of this region. The color of whiskey and with a 14 percent alcohol content, it has a dry flavor quite unlike sake or Western wine. It comes in several grades, depending on the process of fermentation and distillation—ordinary quality, high quality, and special. This yellow rice wine is usually drunk warm like Japanese sake. Shao-sing wine is named after the place where the wine originated, but sometimes the drink is called "yellow wine" in Chinese. Though most Western drinkers find Shao-sing rather tasteless and foreign to their palates, it is a favorite drink among the Chinese and Japanese.

BEGGAR'S CHICKEN

教
化
鸡

Legend has it that a hungry beggar found a chicken at the foot of Lu-shan Mountain. Since he did not have any cooking utensils, he improvised by wrapping the chicken, feathers and all, in mud, and burying it in a bed of hot charcoal. When the chicken was done, the dried mud was broken up and the feathers came off with it.

Since then, innumerable methods have been used to make Beggar's Chicken. In 1882, a special restaurant called Shan Jin Yuan was built at Lu-shan Mountain to serve Beggar's Chicken to the Ching Dynasty Emperor Kuang Hsu (1875–1908). A chef was appointed to improve the preparatory techniques and the flavor. My recipe follows more or less the same method of preparation used in Shan Jin Yuan. Breaking the mud-coated chicken in front of your dinner guests can be very dramatic and impressive. It is a fun dish.

3	large dried lotus leaves
14 to 18	cups of clay
½	cup Shao-sing wine or sake
	Water
1	roasting chicken or fryer, about 3 to 3½ lbs
2	Tbsps Shao-sing wine, sake, or dry sherry
1	Tbsp Szechuan peppercorn salt (see page 40)
2½	Tbsps soy sauce
3	Tbsps oil
1	tsp minced fresh ginger root
2	Tbsps chopped scallion
4	oz lean pork, shredded
½	tsp sugar
½	cup shredded Szechuan preserved vegetable
	String

Soak lotus leaves in hot water for 2 to 3 hours or longer if necessary to soften thoroughly.

In a bucket or a big mixing bowl, mix clay with ½ cup Shao-sing wine and water to the consistency of modeling clay. Set aside.

Wash chicken and pat dry with paper towels. Rub chicken inside and out with 1 Tbsp wine and then rub the outside of the chicken with Szechuan peppercorn salt and 2 Tbsps soy sauce. Set aside for ½ hour or so. Turn chicken over a few times during that period.

Heat 1 Tbsp oil in a wok or a skillet; when it is hot add ginger, scallion, and pork. Stir-fry pork until pinkish color has disappeared. Add the remaining 1 Tbsp wine, and the remaining ½ Tbsp soy sauce, and the sugar and preserved vegetable. Cook and stir until dry. Remove from heat and cool. Preheat oven at 350°

Stuff pork mixture inside the chicken. With the top side facing up, lay out and overlap the lotus leaves making a round surface about 20 inches in diameter. Oil the entire top side of lotus leaves with the remaining oil, using 1 Tbsp oil in all. Wrap chicken up with the lotus leaves, oiled side against the skin, and tie with string.

After spreading the newspapers on the table or floor for protection, coat the chicken with wet clay, and pack clay tightly around the chicken. Place in a roasting pan and bake for 5 hours.

For dramatic effect, use a hammer to break the clay at the dining table in front of guests. Unwrap chicken, place it on a platter, and serve hot. Serves 6 to 8.

醉 鸡 DRUNKEN CHICKEN

This is a handy dish for parties, for it is served cold and can be prepared in advance. The tender meat of Drunken Chicken also makes a good appetizer. The flavor of the fragrant rice wine complements the drinks. When served as an appetizer, following instructions on page 14, bone and cut the meat into bite-sized pieces.

3 lbs chicken (preferably never frozen)
    4 slices of fresh ginger
    2 scallions
    2 Tbsps salt
    1 cup Shao-sing wine or sake (no other substitute)
1½ cups cold chicken stock (from the water after boiling the chicken)

Place chicken in a 4-quart saucepan and fill pan with water just covering the chicken. Add ginger and scallions and bring the water to a boil over high heat. Cover pan, turn heat down to low, and simmer for 45 minutes.

Remove chicken from water. Sprinkle salt all over chicken and sprinkle some inside the cavity. Set aside and let chicken cool thoroughly.

Cut chicken into four quarters with a cleaver or poultry scissors and place in a large bowl. Combine wine and stock and pour over the chicken. Cover and let soak in wine mixture for one to two days in the refrigerator.

Remove chicken from wine and drain. Chop chicken into pieces 2 inches wide and 1 inch long according to instructions on page 13. Arrange the chicken neatly on a plate and serve cold. Serves 6 to 8.

Note: Leftover wine marinade can be stored in the refrigerator for soaking more chicken, if used within a week.

纸 PAPER-WRAPPED
包 CHICKEN
鸡

    1   lb chicken breast
    1   Tbsp Shao-sing wine, sake, or dry sherry
        Dash white pepper
    2   Tbsps soy sauce
    2   Tbsps oyster sauce
    ½   tsp sugar
    1   tsp minced fresh ginger
    3   Tbsps minced scallion
    1   Tbsp sesame oil
30 to 40 6-inch squares of wax paper or cellophane paper
30 to 40 snow peas
    2   cups oil

Cut meat into small pieces about ¼ inch thick, 1 inch wide, and
2 inches long. In a large mixing bowl mix chicken with wine,
pepper, soy sauce, oyster sauce, sugar, minced ginger, minced
scallion, and sesame oil. Let the meat mixture stand for about ½
hour.

Place a square of paper with a point toward you. Lay 2 pieces of
chicken and 1 snow pea along the center diagonal of paper.
Fold nearest point firmly over filling and roll one fold away from
you. Fold right and left corners toward center and make one
more fold away from you. Tuck remaining corner into pocket
created in the folded paper. The result should be a firm, tight
packet about 3 by 1½ inches.

Heat oil in a wok or deep-fryer over moderate heat until oil is
about 350°. Slide 8 to 10 chicken packages into the hot oil with
the tucked side facing up. Fry for 2 minutes. With a strainer,
scoop up the packages and drain. Repeat with the remaining
chicken packages. Arrange packages neatly on a platter with the
tucked side down and serve hot. Serves 6 to 8.

BRAISED CHICKEN WITH CHESTNUTS

栗
子
煨
鸡

8 oz fresh chestnuts, shelled
5 cups water
4 chicken legs
2 Tbsps oil
4 scallions, cut into 2-inch sections
2 slices of ginger, 1 inch in diameter
2 Tbsps Shao-sing wine, sake, or dry sherry
3 Tbsps soy sauce
½ Tbsp sugar
½ Tbsp cornstarch dissolved in 2 Tbsps water

Place shelled chestnuts in a bowl and pour in 4 cups boiling water. Soak for 20 minutes, then peel off the thin layer of tan-colored skin. Set aside.

Rinse chicken and dry with paper towels. Cut each leg through the joint and separate the drumstick and thigh. Chop each drumstick and thigh crosswise against the bone into two equal pieces.

Heat oil in a wok or a heavy saucepan over moderate heat. Drop in scallions, ginger, and chicken; stir and turn the pieces for 1 minute. Add wine, soy sauce, sugar, and the remaining water. Cover and simmer for 15 minutes. Add chestnuts and simmer covered for another 15 minutes. Turn heat to high and allow the liquid to boil rapidly until it has reduced to ½ cup. Stir in dissolved cornstarch and heat until sauce is thickened. Transfer to a plate and serve. This dish can be prepared in advance and reheated. Serves 4 to 6.

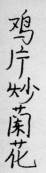

STIR-FRIED CHICKEN WITH BROCCOLI

 8 oz boned chicken breast
½ Tbsp Shao-sing wine, sake, or dry sherry
½ tsp salt
½ Tbsp soy sauce
    Dash white pepper
½ Tbsp cornstarch
½ cup oil (see page 20 on stir-frying)
 3 cups cut-up fresh broccoli
½ cup chicken stock (see page 23)
 1 tsp cornstarch dissolved in 1 Tbsp water

Following instructions on page 16, slice chicken breast into thin pieces about 1 inch wide and 2 inches long. Mix chicken with wine, ¼ tsp salt, and the soy sauce, pepper, and dry cornstarch.

Heat oil in a wok or skillet over medium heat until hot but not smoking. Add chicken, stirring to separate the pieces. Cook for 40 seconds. With a slotted spoon, remove chicken from oil and drain.

Empty all but 1 Tbsp oil from pan; heat oil over high heat. Add broccoli and the remaining ¼ tsp salt. Toss the broccoli for 20 seconds, then add chicken stock. Cover and cook for 2 minutes. Uncover, blend in cooked chicken, and thicken sauce with dissolved cornstarch. Transfer to a plate and serve right away. Serves 4.

CHICKEN STIR-FRIED WITH BEEF

鸡
片
炒
牛
肉

　8　oz boned chicken breast
　6　oz beef, round, heel of round, sirloin, or flank steak
　2　tsps Shao-sing wine, sake, or dry sherry
　⅛　tsp salt
1½　Tbsps cornstarch
　1　egg white
1½　Tbsps soy sauce
　½　Tsp sugar
　　　Dash white pepper
　2　cup chicken stock (see page 23)
　½　cup oil (see page 20 on stir-frying)
　1　large green pepper, seeded and cut into 1-inch
　　　squares
　1　tsp minced ginger

Cut chicken into thin slices, about 1 inch by 2 inches, according to instructions on page 16. Slice the beef against the grain into thin slices approximately the same size as the chicken. In one mixing bowl mix chicken with 1 tsp wine, the salt, ½ Tbsp cornstarch, and ½ egg white. In another mixing bowl mix beef with 1 tsp wine, ½ Tbsp soy sauce, ¼ tsp sugar, ½ Tbsp cornstarch, and the remaining ½ egg white.

In a small bowl combine the remaining soy sauce, sugar, and cornstarch with the white pepper and stock.

Heat oil in a pan over medium heat until hot but not smoking. Drop in chicken, stirring to separate the pieces; cook for 1 minute until meat becomes firm and white. With a slotted spoon, remove chicken from oil and drain. Drop beef into the pan and cook with the remaining oil for 1 minute or until no more pinkish color is visible. Remove beef with slotted spoon and drain. Empty all but 1 Tbsp oil from pan, set over high heat, add green pepper and toss and turn for 30 seconds. Stir in ginger, let cook for 10 seconds, add cooked chicken and beef, then blend in the sauce from the small bowl. When the sauce becomes thick, remove the entire contents from pan and serve at once. Serves 4.

CHICKEN WITH TOMATOES

12 oz chicken meat, white or dark
 1 Tbsp Shao-sing wine, sake, or dry sherry
 ¼ tsp salt
 1 Tbsp cornstarch
 1 small egg white
 1 cup oil (see page 20 on stir-frying)
 3 Tbsps chopped scallion
 2 medium-sized tomatoes, diced
 ¼ cup defrosted frozen green peas
 1 Tbsp soy sauce

Cut chicken meat into thin slices about 1 inch wide and 2 inches long according to instructions on page 13. Mix chicken with wine, salt, cornstarch, and egg white.

Heat oil in a wok until hot but not smoking. Add chicken, stirring to separate the pieces. Cook for 1 minute; with slotted spoon, remove chicken from oil and drain.

Empty all but 1 Tbsp oil from wok. Heat oil over high heat. Add scallion and cook until it becomes slightly brown, then drop in tomatoes and peas. When the tomatoes turn soft, add soy sauce and blend in the chicken. Transfer to a plate. This dish can be cooked in advance and reheated. Serves 4.

STIR-FRIED CHICKEN WITH GREEN BEANS

鸡
肉
青
豆

   8   *oz boneless chicken breast or dark meat*
  ½ *Tbsp Shao-sing wine, sake, or dry sherry*
  ¼ *tsp salt*
  ½ *Tbsp cornstarch*
  1 *small egg white (optional)*
  ½ *cup oil (see page 20 on stir-frying)*
  1 *tsp garlic*
  2 *cups tender green beans, cut into 1½-inch lengths*
  ¼ *cup chicken stock (see page 23)*
  1 *Tbsp soy sauce*

Cut chicken into thin slices about ½ inch wide and 2 inches long. Mix chicken with wine, ⅛ tsp salt, and the cornstarch and egg white (if desired).

Heat oil in a wok or a skillet over moderate heat until hot but not smoking; drop in chicken, stirring to separate the pieces. Cook for 1 minute or until meat becomes firm. Remove chicken with a slotted spoon and drain. Empty all but 1 Tbsp oil from pan, stir in garlic, and cook for 10 seconds; drop in green beans and add the remaining ⅛ tsp salt. Stir-fry for 30 seconds, then add chicken stock and cover pan. Cook for 3 to 4 minutes or longer, depending on the quality of the beans. Uncover pan and add chicken and soy sauce; blend thoroughly with the beans. Transfer to a plate and serve. Serves 4.

STIR-FRIED CHICKEN WITH CABBAGE

鸡
片
包
心
菜

      8 oz boned chicken breast
     ½ Tbsp Shao-sing wine, sake, or dry sherry
     ⅛ tsp salt
     ½ Tbsp cornstarch
      1 small egg white
     ½ cup oil (see page 20 on stir-frying)
     ½ cup firmly packed sliced scallions
      3 cups firmly packed Savoy cabbage (about 8 oz) cut
           into pieces 1 inch by 1½ inches
     ¼ cup chicken stock (see page 23)
      1 Tbsp brown bean sauce, or hot bean sauce, or
           Japanese miso

Cut chicken breast into thin slices, about 1 inch by 1½ inches.
Mix chicken with wine, salt, cornstarch, and egg white.

Heat 1 Tbsp oil in a wok or a skillet over high heat, drop in
scallions and cabbage, and stir for 25 seconds. Add chicken
stock, cover, and cook for 2 minutes. Transfer to a plate. Heat
the remaining oil in a clean wok or skillet over moderate heat
until hot but not smoking; drop in chicken, stirring to separate
the pieces. Cook for 40 seconds; as soon as the chicken becomes white and firm, remove it with a slotted spoon and drain.
Empty all but ½ Tbsp oil from pan and add brown bean sauce,
or hot bean sauce, or Japanese miso. Stir it for 15 seconds, then
add cabbage and chicken and blend thoroughly. Transfer to a
plate and serve. Serves 4.

SCRAMBLED EGGS WITH CHICKEN

蛋
炒
鸡
肉

6 oz boned chicken breast
½ Tbsp Shao-sing wine, sake, or dry sherry
½ Tbsp soy sauce
¼ tsp sugar
½ Tbsp cornstarch
4 Tbsps oil
4 eggs, beaten
¼ tsp salt
  Dash black pepper
2 Tbsps chicken stock (see page 23)
½ cup shredded scallions, or Chinese chives cut into
  1-inch lengths

Cut chicken into thin slices about ¾ inch wide and 1½ inches long. Mix chicken with wine, soy sauce, sugar, cornstarch, and 1 Tbsp oil.

In a bowl combine eggs with salt, pepper, and stock.

Heat the remaining oil in a wok or skillet over moderate heat. Add chicken, stirring to separate the pieces, then add scallions or chives. Stir-fry for about 1 minute; quickly pour in the egg mixture. With a spatula, scramble chicken and eggs until the eggs are set. Transfer to a plate and serve at once. Serves 2 to 4.

CHICKEN WITH CORN SAUCE

栗
米
鸡

Tender, tasty, bite-sized pieces of chicken simmered with sweet creamy corn to produce a very subtle and delicate flavor. A popular dish of recent years, influenced by easy access to both domestic corns and imported canned corns.

> 2 lbs chicken with bones or 1 lb 4 oz boneless
>   chicken meat, either white or dark or both
> 2 Tbsps oil
> 3 Tbsps chopped scallion
> 1 tsp minced ginger
> 2 Tbsps Shao-sing wine, sake, or dry sherry
> 1 cup canned creamed corn
> ½ cup chicken stock (see page 23)
> ½ tsp salt
> ½ Tbsp cornstarch dissolved in 1 Tbsp water

Chop chicken, bones and all, into 1½-inch squares, according to instructions on page 13. If only meat is used, cut into 1-inch squares.

In a heavy saucepan or skillet heat oil over medium heat. Drop in scallion and ginger and stir in hot oil for 20 seconds. Add chicken and with a wooden spoon turn the pieces around until they become slightly brown, about 2 minutes. Add wine, corn, and chicken stock; cover and simmer over low heat for 15 minutes. Uncover, add salt, then thicken the sauce with dissolved cornstarch. Transfer to a plate and serve hot. This dish can be prepared in advance and reheated. Serves 6.

STEAMED CHICKEN WITH FERMENTED BEAN CURD

紅
乳
卤
燕
鸡

This steamed chicken dish is a new creation of chefs from Hangchow. They steam the chicken with fresh bamboo shoots, then garnish it with cooked vegetables that are prepared separately. I simplified the work by steaming the chicken with hard green vegetables like asparagus or broccoli that are just as tasty and also beautiful to look at.

12 oz boneless chicken breast or dark meat
½ Tbsp Shao-sing wine, sake, or dry sherry
⅛ tsp salt
½ Tbsp cornstarch
2 Tbsps mashed fermented red bean curd or
    fermented white bean curd
¼ tsp sugar
1 Tbsp oil
3 Tbsps chopped scallion
1 cup fresh asparagus, cut into 1-inch sections, or 2
    cups broccoli flowerets about 1½ inches long and
    1 inch in diameter
½ Tbsp cornstarch dissolved in 1 Tbsp water

Cut chicken into 1-inch square pieces, about ½ inch thick, according to instructions on page 13. Mix chicken with wine, salt, and cornstarch.

Combine fermented red bean curd with sugar, oil, and scallion; then coat the chicken with the mixture. Put asparagus or broccoli in a shallow bowl or a pie dish. Place chicken on top of the vegetable. Following the instructions on page 21, steam white meat for 10 minutes and dark meat for 15 minutes.

Drain the juices from the bowl into a small saucepan, bring to a boil, and stir in the dissolved cornstarch. Pour sauce over chicken and serve at once. Serves 4.

CHICKEN WINGS WITH MUSTARD SAUCE

芥末鸡翼

This cool, easy-to-assemble dish is a perfect appetizer to serve on a warm day. It is pungent in flavor and crunchy in texture. Boned duck feet are also popular served with this same mustard dressing. Duck feet and chicken wings are both prized for their crunchy texture; if you remove the skin of the wings, you will lose the desired effect. This dish can be prepared hours in advance and served at room temperature.

1½ lbs chicken wings
1 Tbsp Shao-sing wine, sake, or dry sherry
3 scallions, cut into 2-inch sections
3 slices of ginger, about 2 inches in diameter
½ tsp salt
1 Tbsp prepared mustard
½ Tbsp white vinegar
1 tsp sesame oil (optional)

Rinse chicken wings. Pluck or singe off downy feathers, if any. Place chicken wings in a saucepan, add wine, scallions, ginger, salt, and 2 cups water. Bring to a rolling boil, then cover pan and simmer over low heat for 10 minutes. Remove chicken wings from pan and cool.

In a small bowl mix mustard, vinegar, and sesame oil together. Set aside.

Bone cooked chicken wings; tear or cut larger pieces into slivers. Mix chicken slivers with the mustard sauce and serve cold. Serves 4.

BRAISED CHICKEN WINGS WITH HOISIN SAUCE

醬肉爆雞翼

If you like barbecued spareribs, you will like this dish too, with its wonderful combination of sweet, pungent, and spicy flavors. A perfect appetizer, the wings can also be cooked in the oven, but omit the chicken stock if you do. Bake uncovered at 350° for 40 minutes.

10 chicken wings
 2 Tbsps hoisin sauce
 1 Tbsp sesame oil
 1 Tbsp soy sauce
 1 Tbsp oil
 1 tsp minced garlic
 3 Tbsps chopped scallion
 1 Tbsp Shao-sing wine, sake, or dry sherry
 ½ cup chicken stock (see page 23)

Rinse chicken wings and dry with paper towels. Chop off and discard the tip of each chicken wing and cut the remaining sections apart at the joint.

In a small bowl combine hoisin sauce, sesame oil and soy sauce.

Heat oil in a wok or saucepan over moderate heat; drop in garlic and scallion; stir and cook for 20 seconds. Add sauce from the bowl and stir mixture for 20 seconds to bring out the flavor. Add chicken wings, brown and turn the pieces around with the spatula to coat with the sauce. Add wine and stock. Cover and cook for 20 minutes or until no more liquid is left in the pan. Transfer to a plate and serve hot or cold. Serves 4.

醉鸡翼 DRUNKEN CHICKEN WINGS

Drunken chicken wings and other drunken poultry dishes are popular Chinese appetizers. Chicken wings are considered to be the choice part of the bird and are often served at formal dinners and banquets.

> 8 chicken wings (preferably never frozen)
> 3 cups water
> 3 slices of ginger, about 1 inch in diameter
> 2 scallions, cut into 2 sections each
> 1 Tbsp salt
> 1 cup Shao-sing wine or sake (no other substitute)
> 1½ cups cold chicken stock (from the water after
>   boiling the wings)

Rinse chicken wings; chop off and discard the tip of each chicken wing.

In a saucepan bring 3 cups water, ginger, and scallions to a boil. Add chicken wings, immediately bring everything to a rolling boil over high heat. Cover saucepan and reduce heat to low. Poach chicken wings for 15 minutes. Remove chicken wings from liquid and reserve 1½ cups of the broth. Sprinkle salt all over chicken wings and let cool. Place chicken wings in a large bowl. Mix wine with the cold stock, then pour it over the chicken wings. Cover and let soak for at least 24 hours at room temperature.

Remove chicken wings from wine stock and drain. Cut each wing apart at the joint. Place the pieces on a plate and serve cold. Serves 4 to 6.

芋泥鸭 STUFFED TARO ROOT DUCK

Taro root is a tropical bulb vegetable widely used by the Chinese, Japanese, Latin Americans, and Caribbeans in their cooking. The poi of Hawaii is also made from taro root. Other names for taro root are dasheen, tannia, malanga, yautia, and elephant's ear. The skin of taro is dark brown and rough, with rings circling the bulb. When taro is cut open, the flesh is white. After boiling, it becomes light violet or gray with a starchy texture. Taro roots come in various shapes; some are rather small like a new potato, some are tuberous, some almost as large as a small coconut. Any of these varieties are suitable for this recipe. If taro root is unavailable, substitute boiled potatoes.

The boned and stuffed duck is neither greasy nor dry. Best of all, it can be prepared a day in advance as far as the deep-frying stage. It is a perfect first course to serve to your guests at a dinner party.

      1   duck, about 4 lbs
      3   Tbsps soy sauce
      3   cups oil
      2   star anise, whole
      2   scallions, cut into 3-inch sections
      3   slices of ginger, about 1 inch in diameter
      1   Tbsp Shao-sing wine, sake, or dry sherry
      2   cups water
      1   lb taro root
      ½   tsp salt
          Dash black pepper
      4   Tbsps cornstarch
      1   egg white, beaten
      2   Tbsps minced ham (optional)
      1   Tbsp oyster sauce
      ½   tsp sugar
      ½   cup chicken stock (see page 23)
      1   tsp cornstarch dissolved in 1 Tbsp water

Rinse duck and drain. Dry inside and out thoroughly with paper towels. Rub the inside of duck with 2 Tbsps soy sauce and let stand and soak for 30 minutes; drain.

Heat 4 Tbsps of oil in a wok or a large heavy pot over medium heat. Brown the skin of duck until the entire duck becomes golden brown. Add star anise, scallions, ginger, wine, and 2 cups water; cover the pan and simmer over low heat for 1 hour. Remove lid and let the duck cool right in the pot. (You can do all this a couple of days in advance, remove the duck from liquid and discard any spices that cling to it. Store the duck in the refrigerator.)

Peel taro root and cut into small chunks. Place chunks in a steamer or on a plate and steam for 1 hour according to instructions on page 21. Transfer steamed taro root chunks to a bowl and mash; then mix in salt, pepper, 2 Tbsps cornstarch, and the egg white and ham.

Following the instructions on page 14 on how to bone cooked poultry, bone the whole duck. Leave the pieces intact; do not cut them up into bite-sized pieces. Sprinkle them with ½ of the remaining cornstarch. Lay each piece of duck on a flat surface with skin side down and spread a layer of the taro root mixture on top; pack it firmly. Sprinkle both sides of duck with the rest of the cornstarch.

In a small saucepan, combine the remaining Tbsp of soy sauce with oyster sauce, sugar, and stock. Bring to a boil, then thicken with the dissolved cornstarch.

Heat the remaining oil in a wok over medium heat until very hot. Deep-fry the duck pieces, 2 at a time, until golden brown; remove from oil and drain. Repeat with remaining pieces.

Place each piece of duck on a chopping board with skin side up and cut into bite-sized pieces. Slip the knife underneath the duck and transport the pieces to a serving platter. Pour the sauce over the duck and serve at once. Serves 8.

盐水鸭 COLD SALTED DUCK

        1   duck, about 5 lbs
        2   Tbsps Szechuan peppercorns
        ½   Tbsp saltpeter
        5   Tbsps salt
22 to 26   cups water
        ½   Tbsp fennel seeds
        ¼   cup Shao-sing wine sake (no other substitute)
        1   Tbsp sugar
        5   slices of fresh ginger, about 1 inch in diameter
        5   scallions, cut into 3 sections
        1   star anise
        1   cinnamon stick, about 2 inches long

Defrost duck, rinse inside and out thoroughly, and pat dry with paper towels.

Crush Szechuan peppercorns and saltpeter together with mortar and pestle, then mix in 3 Tbsps of salt. Rub duck inside and out with salt mixture. Place duck in a bowl and cover. Refrigerate overnight.

In a large saucepan bring 12 to 14 cups water to a boil over moderate heat. Blanch duck in boiling water for about 2 minutes. Remove duck from the pot, rinse thoroughly with cold water, and drain.

Tie fennel seeds in a piece of cheesecloth. In a large pot bring 10 to 12 cups water, the wine, the remaining 2 Tbsps salt, and the sugar, ginger, scallions, star anise, cinnamon stick, and fennel seeds to a boil. Boil the liquid for 5 minutes, then add the duck. Cover and cook over low heat for 45 minutes. Turn the duck over once during the cooking period. Turn off heat and let the duck cool in the liquid for 3 hours.

Remove duck from pot, reserving the liquid, and chop into 1- by 2-inch pieces according to instructions on page 13. Arrange neatly on a serving plate. Pour ¼ cup of the spiced soaking liquid over duck and serve cold. Serves 6 to 8.

BRAISED DUCK SHANGHAI STYLE

扒
鸭

  1 duck, about 4 lbs or smaller
 10 cups water
  6 Tbsps soy sauce
  4 cups oil
  3 sections of star anise
  ½ tsp Szechuan peppercorns
  3 scallions, cut into 2 or 3 sections
  3 slices of fresh ginger
  2 sections of dried tangerine peel (optional)
  3 Tbsps Shao-sing wine, sake, or dry sherry
  ½ tsp salt
  1 tsp sugar
  3 Tbsps oyster sauce
  1 lb Chinese celery cabbage
  3 Tbsps cornstarch dissolved in ¼ cup water

Defrost duck, wash inside and out under cold running water, and drain. Bring 10 cups of water to a boil and blanch duck in water for a couple of minutes. Dry duck inside and out thoroughly with paper towels. Brush 1 Tbsp soy sauce over the duck and set aside.

Pour oil into a wok or a deep-fryer and heat over high heat until hot. Place duck into hot oil and fry until the skin becomes golden brown. Remove from oil and drain. (Strain oil from wok through a piece of cheesecloth into a bowl or a measuring cup and reuse for cooking other dishes.)

Tie anise and Szechuan peppercorns in a piece of cheesecloth. Put fried duck in a heavy saucepan or dutch oven; add boiling water to cover the duck. Then add scallions, ginger, the bag of anise and peppercorn, and the tangerine peel, wine, the remaining soy sauce, salt, sugar, and oyster sauce. Bring everything to a rolling boil over high heat, cover pan, and reduce heat to low. Simmer duck for 2 hours.

Wash cabbage and cut into 4-inch pieces. After duck has simmered for 2 hours, uncover and skim off most of the oil, then add cabbage, cover, and cook for 5 more minutes.

Take duck out of pan and, if desired, remove the breastbone and backbone.

Place duck on an oval-shaped platter and arrange vegetables around it. Remove ginger, tangerine peel, scallions, and the bag of anise and peppercorn from the sauce. Bring sauce to a rapid boil over high heat, and thicken with dissolved cornstarch. Pour sauce over duck and serve at once. Serves 6 to 8.

BRAISED DUCK IN SESAME OIL SAUCE

     1 duck, about 4 lbs
    12 cups water
     2 slices of ginger, about 1 inch in diameter
    ½ cup soy sauce
    ¼ cup Shao-sing wine, sake, or dry sherry
    ½ Tbsp sugar
    ¼ cup sesame oil

Rinse duck with hot water inside and out. In a large saucepan, bring 12 cups water to a boil. Blanch duck in boiling water for 5 minutes; remove from water and drain.

Place duck in a heavy pot (to prevent the skin from sticking to the bottom, a flat saucer may be placed between the duck and the pot). Add ginger, soy sauce, wine, sugar, and 2 cups of water. Bring everything to a boil, then cover and simmer over low heat for 1½ hours. Baste the duck occasionally with the sauce and turn duck over a couple of times.

Uncover pan and remove the saucer, if you used one. Add sesame oil; cover and cook for 2 more minutes. Remove from heat and cool for 30 minutes.

Chop duck into serving pieces according to instructions on page 13. Arrange the pieces neatly on a plate, then pour the sesame sauce over them. Serve duck warm or cold. Serves 6 to 8.

SOOCHOW SOY SAUCE DUCK

苏
州
卤
鸭

1 duck, about 4 to 5 lbs
1 Tbsp salt
10 cups water
½ cup soy sauce
3 Tbsps Shao-sing wine, sake, or dry sherry
4 slices ginger, about 1 inch in diameter
3 scallions, each one tied into a knot
2 whole star anise, 16 small sections
1 cinnamon stick, about 3 inches long
3 Tbsps rock sugar or 2 Tbsps sugar
1 tsp sesame oil

Rinse duck and drain. Dry duck inside and out with paper towels, then rub the duck inside and out with salt. Let it sit for 4 hours. In a large saucepan bring 10 cups of water to a boil; blanch the duck in boiling water for 5 minutes. Drain all the hot water from saucepan, add all the ingredients except the sesame oil, and then add enough water to cover the duck. Use a saucepan that is just big enough to hold the duck snugly. Bring everything to a boil; cover the pan and cook over moderate heat for 1½ hours. Turn the duck over a couple of times during cooking period.

Remove duck from liquid and let cool to room temperature. Remove and discard all the spices; boil the liquid rapidly over high heat until it reduces to about 1 cup.

Chop duck into serving pieces according to instructions on page 13. Arrange the pieces neatly on a plate, then pour the sesame sauce over them. Serve duck warm or cold. Serves 6 to 8.

 # FIVE-SPICE PIGEONS

    2 pigeons, about 1 lb each
    ½ tsp salt
    1 Tbsp Shao-sing wine, sake, or dry sherry
    3 Tbsps soy sauce
    1 tsp sugar
    2 tsps five-spice powder
    2 Tbsps cornstarch
    3 cups oil

Prepare according to instructions for Five-Spice Quails on page 203. Serves 4.

FIVE-SPICE QUAILS

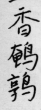

    2 quails, about 1 lb each
    ½ tsp salt
    2 Tbsps Shao-sing wine, sake, or dry sherry
    4 Tbsps soy sauce
    1 tsp sugar
    2 tsps five-spice powder
    2 Tbsps cornstarch
    3 cups oil

Rinse quails with hot water; dry inside and out thoroughly with paper towels. Rub each quail with half of the amount of salt, wine, soy sauce, and sugar. Let stand for ½ hour.

Drain out excess liquid and dry the cavities with paper towels. With a sifter, sprinkle five-spice powder evenly over the outside of each quail, following instructions on page 21, steam the birds for 20 minutes; remove birds from steamer and drain. Sprinkle cornstarch on the inside and outside of each bird. Heat oil in a wok or a deep-fryer until about 350°; deep-fry the quails one at a time for 2–3 minutes each. Remove from oil and drain. According to instructions on page 13 on how to carve cooked poultry, cut up the quails into bite-sized pieces and serve hot. Serves 4.

炒剩餘鸡肉 STIR-FRIED LEFTOVER POULTRY MEAT

This recipe is the answer to what to do with any of your leftover fried chicken, roast duck, or the dark meat of a roast turkey. Or if you live near a Chinatown or a shop that sells Cantonese roast duck, you can whip this dish up with only ½ pound of that delicious and juicy meat. Be sure to include the brownish skin too.

      2 Tbsps oil
      1 cup sliced celery, about ⅛ inch thick and 2 inches
           long
      1 tsp minced ginger
      3 Tbsps chopped scallion
      1 cup thinly torn cooked poultry meat (roast duck,
           fried or baked or roast chicken, or roast turkey)
    1½ Tbsps soy sauce
     ¼ tsp sugar
      1 tsp sesame oil

Heat 1 Tbsp oil in a wok or a skillet over moderate heat. Drop in celery and stir-fry for 30 seconds. Transfer to a plate.

Add the remaining oil to the pan. When it is hot, stir in ginger and scallion. Cook until scallion becomes slightly brown. Drop in poultry meat, then add soy sauce, sugar, and sesame oil. Mix all the ingredients thoroughly and blend in the celery. Transfer to a plate and serve. Serves 2.

CHICKEN FRIED RICE

鸡
丁
炒
饭

The unique feature of this version of chicken fried rice is the initial browning of raw chicken before adding to the rice. The chicken is moist and the rice is flavorful. Moreover, any leftover fried chicken or roast chicken can be used instead of using fresh chicken. Add precooked chicken at the same time that the rice is added.

        6 oz chicken meat, white or dark
        ½ Tbsp Shao-sing wine, sake, or dry sherry
      1½ Tbsps soy sauce
        ½ Tbsp cornstarch
      4½ Tbsps oil
        2 eggs, beaten
        3 Tbsps chopped scallion
        3 cups cooked rice (see page 24)
        ¼ tsp salt
           Dash black pepper
        ⅓ cup defrosted frozen peas

Dice chicken; mix with wine, ½ Tbsp soy sauce, and the cornstarch. Set aside.

Set wok or skillet over high heat. When pan is hot, pour in ½ Tbsp oil. Swirl oil around the pan making sure a large area of the pan is coated. Pour in eggs and quickly swirl eggs around in the pan; as soon as the eggs are set but not completely dry, turn eggs over and cook for a couple of seconds longer. Remove eggs to a plate and cut them into small pieces.

Heat 2 Tbsps oil in the same skillet or wok over high heat, drop in chicken, and stir constantly; cook until chicken becomes firm, about 2 minutes. Remove to a bowl or plate. Heat the remaining oil. When oil is hot, add chopped scallion, stir-fry for a few seconds, then add rice. Stir the rice constantly for about 3 minutes (longer with leftover rice); sprinkle salt and pepper over rice while stirring. Add the remaining soy sauce and the peas and chicken, and fry for another minute. Last, add eggs and mix well with the rice. Remove fried rice from pan and serve. Serves 4 to 6.

鸡饭 VEGETABLE RICE WITH CHICKEN

- 1 recipe basic boiled rice (see page 24)
- 8 oz boned chicken dark meat
- ½ Tbsp Shao-sing wine, sake, or dry sherry
- ½ Tbsp soy sauce
  Dash white pepper
- ½ Tbsp cornstarch
- 3 Tbsps oil
- 3 cups firmly packed bok choy, Swiss chard, Savoy cabbage, or fresh mushrooms, washed and cut into 1-inch squares
- 1 tsp salt

Soak rice according to recipe on page 24. Dice chicken; mix with wine, soy sauce, pepper, cornstarch, 1 Tbsp oil. Set aside.

Heat the remaining oil in a wok or skillet over high heat. Add salt and vegetable and cook for about 2 minutes stirring constantly. The vegetable should be only partially cooked and still very crisp. Set aside.

Set rice over high flame, bring to a rapid boil, and boil for about 2 minutes. Stir in vegetable and the juice, if any; mix the vegetable and the rice thoroughly. Place chicken on top of the rice; cover saucepan and turn heat to low. Cook for 30 minutes. Before serving, blend the chicken with the rice and vegetable. Serves 4.

混 **WONTON SOUP**
饨

½ cup blanched and chopped fresh spinach (see
      instructions below) *
½ lb lean ground chicken
1 Tbsp Shao-sing wine, sake, or dry sherry
1 Tbsp soy sauce
¼ tsp salt
    Dash white pepper
½ Tbsp sesame oil (optional)
40 wonton skins
5 cups seasoned chicken stock (see page 23)
1 to 2 cups fresh spinach, or any leafy green vegetable
    Black pepper

To make the wonton:
Remove any tough stems and wilted leaves from spinach, wash
with cold water, drain. Drop spinach in a pot of boiling water
for a few seconds, just long enough to soften the leaves. Drain
immediately and rinse with cold water. Chop the spinach into
fine pieces; squeeze off the excess water.

In a bowl mix chicken, wine, soy sauce, salt, white pepper, and
sesame oil together, then add chopped spinach and mix everything thoroughly.

Place 1 tsp of filling in the center of each wonton skin and wrap
one by one.

Fill a large saucepan full of water and bring it to a boil, then
drop in the wontons. Bring wontons and water to a boil over
moderate heat. When the water comes to a boil, add 2 cups
cold water and cook slowly for 3 more minutes or until wontons
float to the top. Scoop up wontons with a strainer and drain off
water.

* 2 cups firmly packed spinach or 6 oz fresh spinach yield ½ cup when
blanched.

To make the soup:

While the wontons are being boiled, in another saucepan bring the chicken stock to a boil, add spinach or green vegetables, then the cooked wontons. Remove from heat.

Serve wontons and broth in a big soup bowl all together, or serve in individual small bowls. Sprinkle black pepper on top and serve hot. Serves 6.

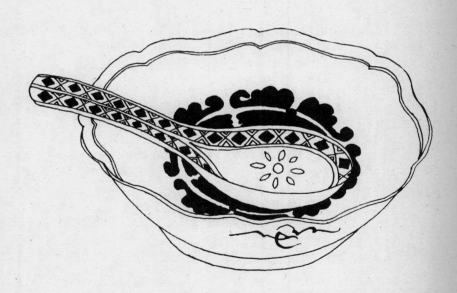

春
卷
EGG ROLLS WITH CHICKEN FILLING

It seems that egg rolls have always represented Chinese food in the United States. They are more popular with American diners than with the Chinese. Even in China the people only recognize egg rolls under the name "spring roll." These delicious, crispy, meat-and-vegetable-filled rolls are generally eaten by people south of the Yangtze River. Egg rolls or spring rolls are popular among the people of Shanghai, Amoy, and Kwangtung, who use egg roll skins much thinner than those found in Chinese restaurants in the States. Both thin and thick egg roll skins are available at Oriental grocery stores. Many supermarkets carry the thick variety.

  ½ *lb boned chicken breast*
  1 *Tbsp Shao-sing wine, sake, or dry sherry*
  2 *Tbsps soy sauce*
    Dash white pepper
  ½ *Tbsp cornstarch*
  3 *cups oil*
  ¼ *lb raw shrimp*
  2 *cups bamboo shoots, shredded*
  1 *cup fresh bean sprouts or shredded celery*
  ¼ *tsp salt*
  ½ *cup chicken stock*
  ½ *tsp sugar*
  1 *Tbsp cornstarch dissolved in 2 Tbsps of water*
 15 *egg roll skins*

To make the filling:

Cut meat into thin slivers. In a bowl mix meat with wine, 1 Tbsp soy sauce, the pepper, ½ Tbsp cornstarch, and 1 Tbsp oil. Set aside.

Shell shrimp, wash, and drain well. Split each shrimp in two lengthwise, then cut them into pea-sized pieces.

Set a wok or skillet over high heat, pour in 2 Tbsps oil. When oil is hot, add chicken. Stir-fry for 1 minute, stir and separate the pieces. Add the shrimp and stir-fry for another minute or until chicken and shrimp become firm. Remove chicken and shrimp to a bowl and set aside.

Set wok back on stove, add another 2 Tbsps oil, and heat over high heat until very hot. Drop in bamboo shoots, add salt. Stir and cook for about 1 minute. Add chicken stock, the remaining 1 Tbsp soy sauce, and the sugar. Add the cooked meat and shrimp and combine all the ingredients thoroughly. Thicken the mixture with dissolved cornstarch. Remove everything from pan to a plate or bowl and cool. The filling can be made a day or two in advance and wrapped without reheating. Mix in the bean sprouts just before wrapping.

To make the egg rolls:

Place 3 Tbsps of filling in the middle of each wrapping and wrap each one into a neat roll about 4 inches long and 1 inch in diameter. This step can be done in advance.

Heat 3 cups oil in a wok or skillet. When oil is hot, drop egg rolls into oil one by one. Fry 4 to 6 rolls at a time for 1 minute when thin wrappings are used, but 2 minutes when thick wrappings are used, or until they become golden brown. Serves 6.

锅贴 SHANGHAI STYLE CHICKEN DUMPLINGS

This is the well-known dumpling dish that sometimes is called pot-stickers or Gwo-tie or Jiao-tz. Generally the boiled dish is called Jiao-tz, while the pan-fried one is called Gwo-tie. The filling can be pork, lamb, chicken, or vegetables; it varies from region to region. The people of Shanghai and Northern China eat these dumplings as a light lunch or snack. I often serve the fried ones as hors d'oeuvres with drinks or as an appetizer at the beginning of a dinner party. The wrappers are readily available in Oriental stores or some supermarkets. The recipe for home-made wrappers is on page 211.

6	oz Chinese celery cabbage or bok choy
6	cups water
12	oz ground chicken, preferably dark meat
½	Tbsp Shao-sing wine, sake, or dry sherry
	Dash white pepper
1	Tbsp soy sauce
¼	tsp salt
⅛	tsp sugar
1	tsp minced ginger
¼	cup chopped scallions
1	Tbsp sesame oil
30	to 35 dumpling wrappers (see page 211)
2	to 4 Tbsps oil
1	cup hot water
3	Tbsps soy sauce
1	Tbsp white vinegar or cider vinegar
¼	tsp chili pepper oil (optional, see page 30)

Separate the cabbage or bok choy into stalks. In a saucepan, bring 6 cups water to a boil, drop in cabbage or bok choy, and blanch for 30 seconds. Remove vegetable from boiling water and rise with cold water until cool. Chop the vegetable very fine. With your hands, squeeze out most of the water.

In a bowl mix chicken with wine, pepper, soy sauce, salt, sugar, ginger, scallions, sesame oil, and the vegetable.

Wrap each dumpling by putting 1 heaping tsp filling in the center of each piece of round thin dough. Fold wrapper over into a half-moon shape and pinch a few pleats firmly along the folded edges.

Set a Teflon or cast-iron skillet over moderate heat. Coat the skillet with 1 Tbsp oil (if cast-iron is used, use 2 Tbsps oil). Arrange dumplings in the pan about 15 to 20 at a time, pleat-side facing up. Pour in ½ cup hot water and cover. Cook for about 5 to 8 minutes or until the liquid has evaporated.

While the dumplings are being cooked, in a small bowl combine 3 Tbsps soy sauce with vinegar and chili pepper oil and set aside.

Uncover pan and fry dumplings for 2 more minutes, or until the bottoms of the dumplings are golden brown. With a spatula, transfer fried dumplings carefully to a plate with the brown side up. Repeat with the remaining dumplings. Serve with the soy sauce and vinegar. Makes about 30 dumplings.

 # Dumpling Wrappers

   2 *cups all-purpose flour*
   ⅔ *cup boiling water for fried and steamed dumplings*
   ½ *cup cold water for boiled dumplings*

Put flour in a bowl and mix in water; work flour and water together until it forms a dough. Knead the dough in the bowl until it becomes smooth. Cover dough with a damp towel or a piece of plastic wrapper and let it set for at least 30 minutes.

Place dough on a floured surface and knead again for 3 minutes.

Form dough into a long sausage-like roll about 1 inch in diameter. Cut dough crosswise into 1-inch pieces. Flatten each piece with the palm of the hand and, with a rolling pin, roll it out into a thin circle about 3 inches in diameter and ⅛ inch thick.

Note: Ready-made dumpling wrappers are available in Oriental grocery stores.

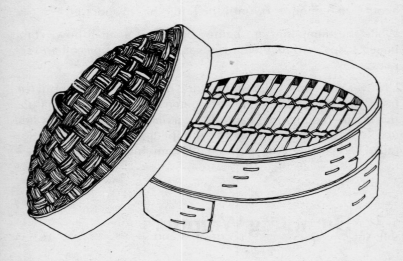

胗 肝 汤 GIBLETS AND RED-IN-SNOW SOUP

> 4 sets chicken or duck giblets, or 1 set turkey giblets
>   (if necks are added, use 1 more cup water)
> 4 cups water
> 2 slices ginger, about 1 inch in diameter
> ½ Tbsp Shao-sing wine, sake, or dry sherry
> 1 scallion, cut into two
> 2 Tbsps red-in-snow pickled mustard greens
> 1 cup diced fresh bean curd
>   Salt to taste
> ½ tsp chili pepper oil (optional; see page 30)
> 1 tsp sesame oil

Remove fat from gizzards; check the inside of each one and peel off yellow lining if any. Rinse thoroughly, then cut gizzards and livers into thin slices.

In a saucepan cover gizzards and hearts with 4 cups water (if necks are used increase the amount of water); add ginger, wine, and scallion. Bring to a rolling boil over high heat, then cover and simmer over low heat for 40 minutes until gizzards and hearts are tender, longer if necks are used. Remove and discard necks; discard ginger and scallion.

Add red-in-snow pickled mustard greens and boil for 5 minutes. Drop in livers and bean curd and bring to a boil. Season with salt; stir in chili pepper oil if desired and sesame oil. Serves 4 to 6.

西 STEAMED CHICKEN
瓜 IN WHOLE
鸡 WATERMELON

The watermelon adds a refreshing taste to the chicken broth and also serves as a bowl for the soup. Quite often the Chinese carve the green surface of the melon skin with intricate designs, making this an attractive and showy party dish. Another good feature of this dish is that it can be prepared half a day in advance.

    1 medium-sized watermelon
   18 cups water
    1 chicken, about 3 lbs
    2 Tbsps Shao-sing wine, sake, or dry sherry
    3 scallions, cut into 3-inch sections
    3 slices of ginger, about 1 inch in diameter
    4 dried Chinese black mushrooms soaked in ½ cup
         warm water
   ¼ cup diced Smithfield ham
    1 cup diced fresh mushrooms
   ½ tsp salt
    1 Tbsp soy sauce

Set the watermelon on its side, then cut a hole out measuring 6 inches wide and 8 inches long on the upper side. Reserve the cut-out piece as a lid. With a tablespoon, scoop out and discard the seeds and the mushy portion of the melon. Carve the green skin with attractive patterns if desired.

In a large saucepan bring 12 cups of water to a boil, blanch chicken in hot water for 2 minutes; remove and drain. Discard the hot water, then place the chicken back into the saucepan. Add 6 cups fresh hot water, wine, scallions, and ginger; cover pan and simmer over low heat for 1 hour.

Remove and discard the stems of the soaked mushrooms, then dice the caps.

Set a low rack in a large oval enamel roasting pan and spread a dish cloth over it, making sure that the cloth is large enough to hang over the edges of the roasting pan. Place the melon on the rack securely. Put the chicken into the melon (if the chicken is too big for the melon, cut the chicken into quarters, then put the pieces into the melon), then add ham and the two kinds of mushrooms and pour in the stock from the saucepan. Place the melon lid over the melon; fill the roasting pan with 3 inches of water. Cover the pan tightly and steam for 30 minutes. Uncover; stir in salt and soy sauce. Using the dish cloth, lift the melon up carefully, support it on a plate or a bowl, and serve. Serves 10.

SZECHUAN AND WEST-CENTRAL CHINA

This section is the heartland of China, lying in the upper reaches of the Yangtze River well into the interior of the country. The land of this river basin is a fertile and heavily populated plain with a humid climate. It is surrounded by tall mountain ranges through which the Yangtze River cuts its famous and spectacular gorges. A Chinese saying that describes this strip of waterway goes: "The road to Szechuan is harder to travel than the road to heaven." Fortunately, through the centuries outsiders have managed to reach Szechuan, and the natives of that region have also been able to travel to other parts of China. With increased social intercourse and commercial contact with people from all over, the cuisine of this otherwise isolated land has spread its reputation and attracted great numbers of devotees from all over the world.

When Szechuan food is mentioned, inevitably we think of the peppery dishes that bring perspiration to our foreheads. Although spiciness is the hallmark of most everyday Szechuan dishes, not all Szechuan food is hot. Banquet dishes are actually rather mild and subtle and not too different from those of the northern regions. The Chicken Liver Custard Soup on page 261 and Szechuan Crispy Duck on page 251 are good examples of their festive cookery.

Of course it is the spiciness of Szechuan cooking that has drawn the attention of diners all over the world. The taste of Szechuan food is dramatic, zestful, and powerful. It is a sensual cuisine that awakens all five senses with its pungent ingredients. Characteristic Szechuan food is often described as hot, sour, salty, sweet, bitter, fragrant, and nutty; all of these features are skillfully blended together into a stimulating and flavorful concoction. A poultry or meat dish is commonly prepared with several different cooking techniques, first marinated with sauces, next steamed, then smoked, and lastly deep-fried. The most-often-used seasonings in making Szechuan dishes are garlic, ginger, scallions, chili peppers, chili oil, soybean paste, soy sauce, sugar, vinegar, Szechuan peppercorns, and sesame oil. It is very typical of Szechuan cooking to use all of these items in the same dish to flavor the principal ingredient, giving the finished production a kaleidoscope of tastes. Even noodles are prepared with a spicy combination of many strong condiments. Wontons are served floating in a bowl of red soup which is colored and spiced by hot chili pepper oil.

One of my all-time favorite Szechuan dishes is steamed meat coated with coarsely ground toasted rice blended with aromatic spices (see page 241 for Steamed Chicken with Aromatic Rice). The meat can be chicken, beef, or pork sliced into very thin morsels. Before steaming, the meat is marinated with wine, soy sauce, chili peppers, and soybean paste, then coated with aromatic rice crumbs. In Szechuan, this dish can only be ordered in small eating places or noodle joints where quick light snacks are served. The meat is steamed and served in small bamboo baskets; even a small eater like myself can put away two to three basketfuls with no difficulty. A chicken version is given in this book, but you can replace the chicken with either pork or beef. In all the spicy dishes in this section the amount of chili peppers can be adjusted to suit your own taste.

辣 油 CHILI PEPPER OIL

Chili pepper oil is available in Oriental grocery stores and at the gourmet sections in some supermarkets. The range of spiciness of ready-made commercial chili oil varies greatly. Most of it looks very red in color yet is quite bland in taste. The degree of hotness of this recipe is just right for all the spicy dishes in this book. Use either more or less as desired.

- ¼ *cup oil*
- 1 *scallion, cut into 2-inch sections*
- 2 *slices of ginger, about 1 inch in diameter*
- ½ *Tbsp ground red pepper (powder)*

In a small saucepan heat oil until almost smoking; add scallion and ginger. Let fry until they turn golden brown, but do not burn. Remove saucepan from heat; pick out and discard scallion and ginger. Allow the oil to cool off for a while. Put ground red pepper in a small bowl, pour in warm oil, and stir until pepper and oil are mixed thoroughly. Let sit until the oil is completely cool. With a piece of cheesecloth, strain the chili oil into a small jar or a bottle. It will keep for a long time in the refrigerator.

宮保鸡丁 GONG BAO JI DING (SPICY CHICKEN WITH PEANUTS)

Gong Bao was the title of a Ching Dynasty official who was dispatched to Szechuan Province as viceroy. While he was stationed in Szechuan, his chef often served this spicy chicken dish to the dinner guests. Because the dish originated from the viceroy's household, people later on named it, too, Gong Bao.

    12 oz boned chicken breast
     1 Tbsp Shao-sing wine or sake
    ¼   tsp salt
     1 Tbsp cornstarch
     1 egg white
    ½   cup raw peanuts
     1 cup oil (see page 20 on stir-frying)
    12 dried chili peppers
     1 tsp minced garlic
     5 scallions, cut into ½-inch sections
     1 Tbsp soy sauce
    ½   tsp sugar
     1 Tbsp wine vinegar

Dice breast meat into ⅓- to ½-inch cubes. In a large bowl mix chicken cubes with wine, salt, cornstarch, and egg white.

Heat oil in a wok over moderate heat until hot, about 325°. Put peanuts into hot oil and fry until they are golden brown; remove from oil and drain.

Heat the oil again until it is hot but not smoking. Drop in the chicken cubes. Stir and separate chicken cubes in oil; when chicken meat turns white and firm, scoop it into a bowl with a slotted spoon and drain.

Empty all but 1 Tbsp of oil from wok. Set wok over heat, drop in chili peppers, garlic, and scallions, and stir-fry them until they become brown and slightly burned. Add the cooked chicken, soy sauce, sugar, and vinegar and stir-fry everything thoroughly for about 1 minute. Drop in peanuts and mix evenly with the other ingredients. Transfer the whole thing to a plate and serve. Serves 4 to 6.

怪
味
鸡
SPICY FANCY-TASTE CHICKEN

The Chinese name for this dish means strange-tasting chicken. The combination of flavors in the sauce is so exotic that even natives of Szechuan have trouble distinguishing all the spices that go into it. This popular Szechuan appetizer is also one of my favorite cold dishes. It is easy and simple, a perfect dish for a buffet or picnic.

1   chicken breast about 1 lb, or ½ chicken about 1½ lbs
½   Tbsp chili pepper oil (see page 30) or Tabasco sauce
½   tsp toasted ground Szechuan peppercorn powder (see page 40)
2   Tbsps soy sauce
¼   tsp sugar
1   Tbsp vinegar
½   Tbsp sesame oil
1   Tbsp chopped scallion
1   tsp minced ginger
1   tsp minced garlic
¼   cup chopped roasted peanuts (optional)

Fill a 2-quart pan with 2 inches of water and set over medium heat. Put the chicken into the water and cover the pan. Bring to a boil and then turn the heat down to low; simmer chicken for 20 minutes. Remove chicken from water and cool.

When chicken is cold, bone and cut it into 1-inch squares according to instructions on page 15; arrange chicken neatly on a platter.

In a small bowl combine chili pepper oil, Szechuan peppercorn powder, soy sauce, sugar, vinegar, sesame oil, scallion, ginger, and garlic. Pour sauce over chicken, then sprinkle chopped peanuts on top. Serves 4.

DICED CHICKEN WITH CHILI PEPPER

辣
子
鸡
丁

```
12  oz chicken breast, diced
 ¼  tsp salt
  1  Tbsp Shao-sing wine, sake, or dry sherry
  1  Tbsp cornstarch
  1  small egg white
  1  Tbsp soy sauce
 ½  tsp sugar
 ½  Tbsp vinegar
  2  Tbsps chicken stock (see page 23) or water
  1  cup oil (see page 20 on stir-frying)
  1  tsp minced ginger
 ½  tsp minced garlic
  2  Tbsps chopped scallion
  2  Tbsps chopped fresh chili pepper or ½ Tbsp dried
        red pepper flakes
 ½  cup diced water chestnuts
```

Mix chicken with salt, ½ Tbsp wine, and the cornstarch and egg white.

In a small bowl combine soy sauce, sugar, vinegar, stock, and the remaining ½ Tbsp wine.

Heat oil in a wok over moderate heat until hot but not smoking. Drop in chicken, stir to separate the pieces, and cook until meat becomes white and firm, about 1 minute. With a slotted spoon, remove chicken from oil and drain. Empty all but 1 Tbsp oil from wok, add ginger, garlic, scallion, and chili pepper; stir and cook for about 30 seconds. Add cooked chicken and water chestnuts, then stir in the soy sauce mixture from the bowl. Mix everything thoroughly, coating the chicken with the spices and sauce. Transfer to a plate and serve. This dish can be prepared in advance and reheated in the microwave oven. Serves 4.

SPICY CHICKEN WITH LEEKS

家常鸡条

12 oz boned chicken or turkey breast
¼ tsp salt
1 Tbsp Shao-sing wine, sake, or dry sherry
4 tsps cornstarch
1 small egg white
½ Tbsp soy sauce
½ tsp sugar
½ Tbsp vinegar
¼ cup chicken stock (see page 23)
1 cup oil (see page 20 on stir-frying)
2 cups leeks sliced in 1-inch lengths
1 tsp minced ginger
1 Tbsp chopped fresh chili pepper or 1 tsp dried red
      pepper flakes
1 Tbsp hot bean paste

Cut chicken into strips about 2 inches long and ¼ inch wide.
Mix chicken with salt, ½ Tbsp wine, 3 tsps cornstarch, and the
egg white. In a small bowl combine soy sauce, the remaining
wine, sugar, vinegar, stock, and the remaining 1 tsp cornstarch.

Heat oil in a wok over moderate heat until hot but not smoking.
Drop in chicken, stir to separate the pieces, and cook until meat
becomes white and firm, about 1 minute. With a slotted spoon,
remove chicken from oil and drain. Empty all but 1 Tbsp oil
from wok, reserve the rest; set wok over high heat; drop in leeks
and stir-fry for 2 minutes or until leeks turn soft, then transfer to
a plate. (Add 2 to 4 Tbsps water to leeks while cooking if they
become dry.) Add 1 Tbsp reserved oil to wok, stir in ginger, chili
pepper, and hot bean paste. Cook for 20 seconds, then add
chicken and the soy sauce mixture. When sauce is thickened,
blend in leeks. Transfer to a plate and serve. Serves 4.

棒棒鸡 BON BON CHICKEN (COLD CHICKEN WITH SPICY SESAME PASTE SAUCE)

Don't let your French mislead you. This dish is not at all sweet, but rather spicy with a delightful blend of sesame paste mixed with soy sauce, vinegar, sesame oil, ginger, and scallion. "Bon Bon," meaning sticks or clubs in Chinese, refers to the shredded chicken meat.

12 oz chicken breast with ribs
1 oz mung bean noodles (about 1 cup after soaking)
2 cups hot water
1 medium-sized cucumber
3 Tbsps toasted sesame paste, tahini, or peanut butter
3 Tbsps water
2 Tbsps soy sauce
1 Tbsp vinegar
½ tsp sugar
1 Tbsp hot chili pepper oil (see page 30) or chili paste
    or combine ½ Tbsp hot chili pepper oil and ½
    Tbsp chili paste
1 tsp minced ginger
1 Tbsp chopped scallion
½ Tbsp sesame oil

Steam chicken for ½ hour according to instructions on page 21, or poach it in boiling water for 15 minutes. Cool and chill in the refrigerator for 2 hours.

Soak mung bean noodles in 2 cups hot water for ½ hour, drain, and set aside.

Peel the cucumber and cut it in two lengthwise; remove the seeds. Shred cucumber into very fine slivers.

In a bowl mix sesame paste with 3 Tbsps water, soy sauce, and vinègar until it becomes thin and smooth. Add sugar, chili pepper oil, ginger, scallion, and sesame oil; mix all the ingredients thoroughly. Set aside.

Bone chicken according to directions on page 15 and then tear the meat into thin slivers. Arrange cucumber in the center of a serving plate, put soaked mung bean noodles on top, then the chicken on top of the noodles. Pour spicy sesame paste sauce over chicken just before serving. This dish can be prepared in advance. Store in the refrigerator and bring to room temperature to serve. Serves 4 to 6.

FRIED CHICKEN WITH SZECHUAN PEPPERCORN SAUCE

花椒鸡

This aromatic dish combined with a spicy sauce is pungent in flavor and slightly chewy in texture. It can be served either warm immediately from the stove to the table or cold as an appetizer. In Szechuan, common ingredients prepared in the same way include pork, beef, rabbit, fish, and wild game. I find turkey is another suitable substitute.

1 lb chicken meat, dark or white
1 Tbsp Shao-sing wine, sake, or dry sherry
2 Tbsps soy sauce
½ cup sliced scallions
4 slices of ginger, about 1 inch in diameter
1 Tbsp cornstarch
1 cup oil
2 Tbsps sesame oil
1 Tbsp Szechuan peppercorn
½ Tbsp dried red pepper flakes
½ Tbsp minced ginger
3 Tbsps finely chopped scallion
½ tsp sugar
1 Tbsp vinegar
2 Tbsps chicken stock (see page 23)

Cut chicken into strips about ½ inch thick and 2 inches long. Marinate chicken with wine, 1 Tbsp soy sauce, sliced scallions, and ginger for 1 hour. Drain until dry; discard ginger and scallions. Mix chicken with cornstarch.

Heat oil in a wok or a deep-fryer over high heat; when oil is smoking, add chicken. Stir immediately to separate the strips. Fry until the strips become dry and golden brown. With a strainer, remove chicken from oil and drain.

Empty all the oil from the wok. Heat sesame oil in wok over moderate heat until hot. Drop in Szechuan peppercorns and fry until they become dark brown; remove with slotted spoon and discard. Add dried red pepper flakes, minced ginger, and chopped scallion and fry for 30 seconds or until pepper flakes turn black. Stir in chicken, remaining soy sauce, sugar, vinegar, and chicken stock. Cook and stir until there is no more liquid. Transfer to a plate and serve hot or cold as desired. Serves 6.

碎米鸡丁 SPICY DICED CHICKEN WITH PEANUT CRUMBS

12 oz boned chicken breast
 2 tsps Shao-sing wine, sake, or dry sherry
¼ tsp salt
1⅓ Tbsps cornstarch
 1 small egg white
 1 Tbsp soy sauce
 1 Tbsp vinegar
½ tsp sugar
 1 cup oil (see page 20 on stir-frying)
 1 Tbsp chopped fresh hot chili pepper or ½ Tbsp
       dried red pepper flakes
 1 tsp minced garlic
 1 tsp minced ginger
 2 Tbsps chopped scallion
½ cup sliced water chestnuts
¼ cup finely chopped shelled plain roasted peanuts

Dice breast meat into ½-inch cubes. Mix chicken with wine, salt, 1 Tbsp cornstarch, and the egg white.

In a small bowl combine soy sauce, vinegar, sugar, and the remaining ⅓ Tbsp cornstarch.

Heat oil in a wok over moderate heat until hot but not smoking. Drop in chicken; stir and separate the cubes in oil. When chicken turns white and firm, in about 1 minute, remove with a slotted spoon and drain.

Empty all but 1 Tbsp oil from wok; drop in chili pepper, garlic, ginger, and scallion. Stir them in hot oil for 20 seconds, add cooked chicken, water chestnuts, and the soy sauce mixture from the bowl. Blend everything thoroughly, then transfer to a plate and sprinkle peanut crumbs on top. Serve at once. Serves 4.

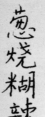

SPICY CHICKEN WINGS WITH SCALLIONS

This spicy Szechuan-style chicken dish is rich with a pungent flavor. The oil is first seasoned with Szechuan peppercorns and dried hot chili peppers, then more spices are added to enrich the sauce. You can substitute turkey or chicken meat cut in cubes for the chicken wings. A good party dish, because it can be prepared in advance.

- 10   chicken wings, or 1 lb chicken or turkey meat
- 2   Tbsps oil
- 1   tsp Szechuan peppercorns
- 10   dried hot chili peppers, each about 1 inch long, with seeds removed and the peppers broken into small pieces.
- 2   Tbsps chopped scallion
- 3   slices ginger, about 1 inch in diameter
- 1   Tbsp Szechuan hot bean paste or brown bean paste
- 1½   Tbsps soy sauce
- 1   Tbsp Shao-sing wine, sake, or dry sherry
- 1   tsp sugar
- 2   Tbsps cider vinegar
- ½   cup chicken stock (see page 23)
- 1   cup scallions, cut into 1½-inch sections

Rinse chicken wings, remove fine feathers, if any, and dry with paper towels. Chop off and discard the tip of each chicken wing and cut the remaining sections apart at the joint.

Heat 1 Tbsp oil in a wok or saucepan over moderate heat; drop in peppercorns and chili peppers. Cook them slowly until they become black, then with a slotted spoon remove them from oil and discard. Add chopped scallion and ginger to the spiced oil, stir them for 10 seconds; drop in chicken wings and brown them over high heat. Mix in hot bean paste, soy sauce, wine, sugar, vinegar, and stock. Cover and simmer over moderate heat for 10 minutes.

While the wings are being cooked, in another pan heat the remaining 1 Tbsp oil and stir-fry the scallion sections for 2 minutes or until they become slightly brown.

Uncover saucepan or wok, add scallion sections to the chicken wings. Cover pan and simmer for 2 more minutes. Transfer to a platter and serve. Serves 4 to 6.

YU-XIANG CHICKEN GIZZARDS

魚
香
曰
鸡
臀

2   Tbsps dried tree ears
1   cup hot water
1   lb chicken gizzards, duck gizzards, or turkey
      gizzards
1   Tbsp salt
1   Tbsp soy sauce
½   tsp sugar
1   Tbsp vinegar
1   tsp sesame oil
½   Tbsp Shao-sing wine, sake, or dry sherry
1   tsp cornstarch
2   Tbsps oil
¼   cup chopped scallions
½   Tbsp minced ginger
½   Tbsp minced garlic
1   Tbsp hot bean paste
1   Tbsp chopped fresh chili peppers or ½ tsp dried
      pepper flakes
¼   cup finely chopped water chestnuts (optional)

Soak dried tree ears in 1 cup hot water for 30 minutes. Rinse thoroughly, remove sand and tough woody tips. Tear or cut the tree ears into smaller pieces.

Remove fat from gizzards, check the inside of each one and remove yellow lining if any. Rinse gizzards thoroughly with salted water, or rub them with 1 Tbsp salt and rinse. Cut each gizzard crosswise into pieces about ¼ inch thick.

In a small bowl combine soy sauce, sugar, vinegar, sesame oil, wine, and cornstarch.

Heat oil in a wok or a skillet over high heat. Stir in scallions, ginger, and garlic, cook for 20 seconds; add hot bean paste, chili peppers or dried pepper flakes, and gizzards. Stir and turn the gizzards continuously for 2 minutes; pour in soy sauce mixture from the bowl, add tree ears and water chestnuts. Stir and blend everything together. When sauce becomes thick, transfer to a plate and serve. Serves 4 to 6.

蒸辣椒鸡块 CHICKEN STEAMED WITH HOT BEAN PASTE

12 oz chicken meat, white or dark
½ Tbsp Shao-sing wine, sake, or dry sherry
⅛ tsp salt
½ Tbsp cornstarch
1 Tbsp oil
1 tsp garlic
1½ Tbsps Szechuan hot bean paste
¼ tsp sugar

Cut chicken meat into pieces ⅔ inch by 1½ inches; mix with wine, salt, and cornstarch. Place chicken in a shallow bowl or a pie dish.

Heat oil in a small saucepan over moderate heat. Add garlic, stir for 5 seconds in hot oil, then mix in hot bean paste and sugar. Cook and stir for 20 seconds, pour sauce over chicken, and mix well.

According to the instructions on page 21, steam white meat for 10 minutes and dark meat for 15 minutes. Serves 4.

八宝鸭 EIGHT PRECIOUS DUCK

The Chinese believe there are eight lucky objects; some bring good fortune and happiness while some drive away evil spirits. These eight items are: a pearl to guard against the evils of fire; a mirror to reflect away images of ghosts; a coin with a square hole for prosperity; a lozenge signifying victory or success; a jade chime symbolizing felicity; two books bound together as protection against witchcraft; a fragrant artemisia leaf for its power to disperse demons; a rhinoceros horn as a symbol of happiness. By extension, the term "eight precious" represents the concept of these original eight things and is an auspicious title for the dish.

> 1 duck, about 4 lbs
> 1 cup glutinous rice
> 6 cups cold water
> 4 dried scallops or 1 Tbsp dried shrimp
> 1 cup hot water
> 6 dried Chinese black mushrooms, about 1½ inches
>   in diameter
> ¼ cup dried lotus seeds or 1 cup quartered chestnuts
> ¼ cup barley
> 2 Tbsps oil
> ¼ lb lean pork, diced
> 1 duck gizzard, washed and diced (optional)
> 1 duck liver, washed and diced (optional)
> 1 Tbsp Shao-sing wine or sake
> ¼ cup diced Smithfield ham or ¼ cup diced Chinese
>   sausage
> 1 tsp salt
> 2 Tbsps soy sauce
> ½ tsp sugar
> ⅛ tsp white pepper

6 slices of fresh ginger
3 scallions, cut into sections
soy sauce (optional)
cornstarch (optional)
5 cups oil (optional)

Bone the duck and remove the whole carcass, according to instructions on page 14 on how to bone poultry whole. This step can be done a day in advance.

Soak glutinous rice with 3 cups cold water for 2 hours. Drain.

In small bowl pour ½ cup hot water over dried scallops or dried shrimp and soak for 1 hour. Tear scallops into small pieces and save the water.

Pour the remaining hot water over mushrooms and soak for ½ hour, then cut them into pea-sized pieces.

Soak lotus seeds in 1 cup cold water for a couple of hours, then transfer to a small saucepan and cook over low heat until tender; drain.

In small bowl soak barley in 1 cup cold water for a couple of hours and drain.

Set a wok or a large saucepan over moderate heat, pour in oil. When oil is hot, add pork, gizzard, and liver and stir-fry for a minute, or until meat changes color. Add wine, scallops, mushrooms, and the glutinous rice. Pour in reserved scallop water and the remaining cup of water; bring the liquid to a rolling boil. Stir rice with a spoon and mix well with the other ingredients. Cover pan tightly, turn the heat to low, and cook for 30 minutes. After 30 minutes, turn heat off and let the rice rest undisturbed for 20 minutes. Uncover, fluff rice up with chopsticks, mix in ham, lotus seeds, barley, salt, soy sauce, sugar, and pepper. Mix everything thoroughly and allow the rice stuffing to cool.

Pack the stuffing into the cavity of the duck. Close up.the neck and tail openings with trussing pins or needle and thread. Shape the body of the duck back into the original shape.

Place duck on a plate and arrange ginger and scallions on top of the duck. Put the duck and plate in a large pan over boiling water, or in a steamer. Cover pan tightly and steam on moderate heat for 2 hours. Discard ginger and scallions. The duck can be served as it is, and carved into small portions at the table. Or, if you prefer a crispy skin, allow duck to cool for a couple of hours, brush soy sauce all over the duck, then sprinkle with cornstarch. In a wok or deep-fryer heat 5 cups oil until very hot; deep-fry duck until it becomes golden brown. Remove from oil and drain. Place duck on a serving plate and cut into small portions at the table. Serves 6 to 8.

贵 EMPRESS CHICKEN
妃 (BRAISED CHICKEN WINGS
鸡 WITH MUSHROOMS)

10 medium-sized Chinese mushrooms
 1 cup hot water
10 chicken wings
 6 cups cold water
 3 Tbsps oil
 4 slices of fresh ginger, about 1 inch in diameter
 5 scallions, cut into 2-inch sections
 2 Tbsps Shao-sing wine, sake, or dry sherry
 1 tsp sugar
 3 Tbsps soy sauce
 1 cup chicken stock or water (see page 23)
 ½ cup sliced bamboo shoots
 ½ Tbsp cornstarch dissolved in 1 Tbsp of water
      (optional)

Soak mushrooms in 1 cup hot water for 30 minutes. Wash off sand and remove and discard stems; cut each in two.

Wash chicken wings, chop off the tip end of each wing, then cut the remaining sections apart at the joint. Bring 6 cups water to a boil, drop in the chicken wings, blanch for a few seconds, drain, and dry thoroughly with paper towels.

Set a heavy saucepan on medium heat and pour in oil. When oil is hot, add ginger and scallions, stir for a few seconds, then add chicken wings. Cook chicken wings until slightly brown, then add wine, sugar, soy sauce, stock, mushrooms, and bamboo shoots. Bring everything to a boil and cover the pan. Lower the heat and let simmer for 15 minutes. If there is too much sauce, turn heat to high and boil the sauce rapidly until most is evaporated, or thicken it with the dissolved cornstarch. This dish can be prepared in advance and reheated. Serves 4.

SZECHUAN CRISPY CHICKEN LEGS

香酥鸡腿

6 chicken legs, thigh and drumstick joint together
½ Tbsp star anise
1 Tbsp Szechuan peppercorns
6 scallions, crushed and cut into 2-inch sections
8 slices of ginger about 1 inch in diameter, crushed
2 Tbsps Shao-sing wine, sake, or dry sherry
2 Tbsps salt
2 Tbsps soy sauce
1 tsp sugar
1 tsp five-spice powder
1 Tbsp cornstarch
3 cups oil

Rinse chicken legs and dry them with paper towels.

Crush star anise with mortar and pestle. Mix star anise, Szechuan peppercorns, scallions, ginger, wine, and salt together, then rub chicken legs with the mixture. Pack the chicken legs in a glass bowl or baking dish. Cover and marinate for 8 hours or overnight in the refrigerator. Turn the pieces over once during marinating period.

Mix 1 Tbsp soy sauce with sugar and five-spice powder. Coat the chicken legs thoroughly with the mixture.

Place chicken legs in a shallow bowl and steam over high heat according to instructions on page 21 for 45 minutes. Drain off the liquid from the bowl; remove and discard ginger, scallions, peppercorns, and star anise. Let cool and dry for at least 2 hours.

Brush the remaining soy sauce over chicken legs, then sprinkle cornstarch over them. Heat oil in a wok or a deep-fryer until very hot, fry 2 to 3 legs at a time until crisp and brown, remove, and drain. Chop each leg crosswise into 4 pieces, or just cut through the joint into 2 pieces. Arrange on a plate and serve. Serves 4 to 6.

STEAMED CHICKEN WITH AROMATIC RICE

½ lb chicken meat, white or dark
½ Tbsp Shao-sing wine, sake, or dry sherry
½ Tbsp soy sauce
½ tsp sugar
1 Tbsp hot bean paste
1 tsp dried red pepper flakes
1 Tbsp sesame oil
⅓ cup defrosted peas
½ cup aromatic rice crumbs (see below)
4 slices of ginger, about 1 inch in diameter
2 scallions, cut into ½-inch sections

Cut chicken into thin slices about 1 inch wide by 2 inches long. Marinate chicken for 20 minutes with wine, soy sauce, sugar, hot bean paste, red pepper flakes, and sesame oil.

Coat chicken and peas with aromatic rice crumbs, then mix in ginger and scallions. Place chicken and peas in a shallow bowl and steam for 30 minutes according to instructions on page 21. Remove bowl from steamer and serve at once. Serves 4.

Aromatic Rice Crumbs

½ cup raw rice
½ tsp five-spice powder

In an ungreased frying pan, toast rice over a low flame for 10 minutes or until rice becomes light brown. Crush rice with mortar and pestle or blend in an electric blender at medium speed for 2 minutes until it becomes fine crumbs. Mix in the five-spice powder.

SPICY CHENGTU CHICKEN

成都鸡

12 oz boned chicken or turkey breast
1 Tbsp Shao-sing wine, sake, or dry sherry
¼ tsp salt
1 Tbsp cornstarch
1 small egg white
1 Tbsp soy sauce
½ tsp sugar
½ Tbsp vinegar
2 Tbsps chicken stock (see page 23) or water
½ Tbsp sesame oil
¼ tsp Szechuan peppercorn powder (see page 40)
1 cup oil (see page 20 on stir-frying)
½ cup diced celery (optional)
3 Tbsps chopped scallion
1 Tbsp minced ginger
1 Tbsp minced garlic
1 Tbsp hot bean paste
2 Tbsp coarsely chopped pickled red pepper

Cut chicken or turkey into pieces ½ inch wide by ¼ inch thick by 1½ inches long. Mix chicken or turkey with ½ Tbsp wine and the salt, cornstarch, and egg white.

In a small bowl combine soy sauce, sugar, vinegar, stock, sesame oil, Szechuan peppercorn powder, and the remaining wine.

Heat oil in a wok over moderate heat until hot but not smoking. Drop in chicken or turkey, stir to separate the pieces; cook until meat becomes firm, about 1 minute. With a slotted spoon, remove meat from oil and drain. If celery is used, drop it into the oil and cook for 20 seconds, remove, and drain. Empty all but 2 Tbsps oil from wok, set over high heat, add scallion, ginger, garlic, hot bean paste, and pickled pepper; stir and cook for about 20 seconds. Add chicken or turkey, celery (if used), and soy sauce mixture from the bowl; blend everything together. Transfer to a serving plate and serve. This dish can be prepared in advance and reheated in the microwave oven. Serves 4.

SPICY HOME-STYLE KWAICHOW CHICKEN

家庭贵州鸡

1 lb chicken breast, light or dark meat
1 Tbsp Shao-sing wine, sake, or dry sherry
¼ tsp salt
2 Tbsps soy sauce
1 tsp sugar
1 Tbsp sesame oil
3 Tbsps oil
   Dried chili peppers, about 10 to 12 small ones
1 tsp Szechuan peppercorns
3 scallions
4 slices of ginger, about 1 inch in diameter
1 cinnamon stick
1 star anise or eight small sections
½ cup chicken stock (see page 23)

Cut chicken into ¾-inch squares. In a small bowl combine wine, salt, soy sauce, sugar, and sesame oil.

Heat oil in a wok over moderate heat until hot, add chili peppers and cook until they turn dark brown, then drop in Szechuan peppercorns. Fry peppercorns for 10 seconds, then add chicken, scallions, and ginger. With a spatula, stir-fry chicken until the meat becomes firm, about 1 minute. Add cinnamon stick, star anise, stock, and the soy sauce mixture from the bowl; cover and simmer over low heat for 15 minutes. Uncover; discard ginger, star anise, and cinnamon stick. Transfer chicken to a plate and serve. This dish can be prepared in advance and reheated. Serves 4.

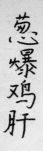

STIR-FRIED CHICKEN LIVERS WITH SCALLIONS

10 oz chicken livers
½ Tbsp Shao-sing wine, sake, or dry sherry
¼ tsp salt
  Dash of white pepper
 1 Tbsp cornstarch
 1 Tbsp soy sauce
½ Tbsp vinegar
½ Tbsp sesame oil
 1 tsp sugar
12 good-sized scallions
 1 cup oil
 6 slices of ginger, 1 inch in diameter
 1 Tbsp minced garlic
 1 Tbsp chopped fresh chili pepper or 1 tsp dried red
     pepper flakes

Cut chicken livers into strips ½ inch thick, then mix with wine, salt, pepper, and cornstarch.

In a small bowl combine soy sauce, vinegar, sesame oil, and sugar.

Rinse scallions and split each stalk lengthwise to separate the layers. Then cut them crosswise into 1½-inch lengths.

Heat oil in a wok over high heat until very hot. Drop in livers; stir to separate the strips.

(*Caution:* When deep-frying chicken livers, protect your arms from oil splatter by wearing long sleeves and standing a couple of feet away from the pan.)

Cook until firm with no trace of red color, about 2 minutes. With a slotted spoon, remove livers from oil and drain. Empty all but 2 Tbsps oil from wok. Add scallions and ginger, and toss and turn until scallions become soft. Drop in garlic and chili pepper and stir them in hot oil for 10 seconds. Return liver to wok and and mix in the soy sauce mixture from the bowl. Blend everything thoroughly, transfer to a serving plate, and serve at once. Serves 4.

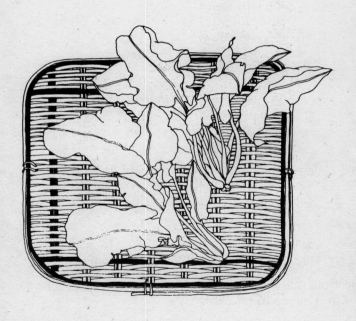

回锅火鸡片 TWICE-COOKED TURKEY

This is not a traditional Szechuan dish but rather an adaptation of the well-known Twice-cooked Pork, and a handy recipe to have right after Thanksgiving, when you can't stand another cold turkey sandwich. Those leftover bits and pieces of dark turkey meat can be transformed into an exciting new dish—so easy and so tasty. Serve it with either rice or bread.

    2 Tbsps oil
    1 large green pepper, seeded and cut into 1-inch
         squares
    1 cup sliced leek or scallions
    1 tsp minced garlic
    1 tsp minced ginger
    ½ Tbsp sweet bean paste
    1 Tbsp Szechuan hot bean paste
    1 Tbsp Shao-sing wine, sake, or dry sherry
    ½ Tbsp soy sauce
    ½ tsp sugar
    1 cup firmly packed cooked turkey meat, cut into
         pieces about ¼ inch thick by 1 inch wide by 2
         inches long (smaller pieces will work just as well)
    ¼ cup chicken stock (see page 23)

Heat 1 Tbsp oil in a wok or skillet; drop in green pepper. Stir and toss for 1 minute, then add leek and stir-fry both ingredients for 1 more minute or till the leek becomes soft. Remove vegetables to a dish.

Heat the remaining oil. Stir in garlic and ginger and cook for 15 seconds. Add sweet bean paste, hot bean paste, wine, soy sauce, sugar, and turkey. Blend and mix the ingredients for 1 minute. Add green pepper, leek, and stock; combine everything thoroughly. Transfer to a plate and serve. Serves 2 to 3.

YU-XIANG SPICY TURKEY STRIPS

魚
香
火
鸡

Yu-xiang dishes are the specialties of Szechuan Province. A direct translation of *yu-xiang* is fish-fragrant or fish-flavor. Yu-xiang sauce is a mixture of chili pepper paste, hot bean paste, garlic, ginger, scallions, chopped tree ears, soy sauce, and vinegar. The sauce, originally used for flavoring fish dishes, now is applied to all kinds of meats and vegetables.

  2   *Tbsps dried tree ears*
  1   *cup hot water*
 12   *oz turkey or chicken meat, either dark or white*
 ¼   *tsp salt*
1½   *Tbsps Shao-sing wine, sake, or dry sherry*
  4   *tsps cornstarch*
  1   *small egg white*
  1   *Tbsp soy sauce*
 ½   *tsp sugar*
  1   *Tbsp vinegar*
  1   *tsp sesame oil*
  1   *cup oil (see page 20 on stir-frying)*
  3   *Tbsps chopped scallion*
 ½   *Tbsp minced ginger*
 ½   *Tbsp minced garlic*
  1   *Tbsp chopped fresh chili pepper or ½ tsp dried red pepper flakes*
  1   *Tbsp hot bean paste*
 ¼   *cup finely chopped water chestnuts*

Soak dried tree ears in hot water for 30 minutes. Rinse thoroughly, remove sand and tough woody tips.

Cut turkey meat into strips about 2 inches long and ¼ inch wide. Mix turkey with salt, 1 Tbsp wine, 3 tsps cornstarch, and the egg white.

In a small bowl combine soy sauce, sugar, vinegar, sesame oil, and the remaining wine and cornstarch.

Heat oil in a wok over moderate heat until hot but not smoking. Drop in turkey, stirring to separate the strips; cook until meat becomes firm, about 1 minute. With a slotted spoon, remove turkey from oil and drain. Empty all but 2 Tbsps oil from wok, set over high heat, add scallion, ginger, garlic, chili pepper, and hot bean paste; stir and cook for about 20 seconds. Add water chestnuts, tree ears, turkey, and the soy sauce mixture from the bowl; stir and blend everything together. When sauce becomes thick, transfer the entire contents to a serving plate and serve. This dish can be prepared in advance and reheated. Serves 4.

SPICY TURKEY WITH SESAME OIL

1 lb boned turkey breast
1 Tbsp Shao-sing wine, sake, or dry sherry
3 Tbsps soy sauce
3 Tbsps cornstarch
1 Tbsp vinegar
2 Tbsps sesame oil
½ tsp sugar
2 cups oil
3 Tbsps coarsely chopped fresh chili pepper
½ tsp Szechuan peppercorns, crushed
¼ cup chopped garlic leaves or scallions

Dice turkey into ½-inch cubes. Mix turkey with wine, 1 Tbsp soy sauce, and the cornstarch.

In a small bowl combine the remaining soy sauce with vinegar, sesame oil, and sugar.

Heat oil in a wok over moderate heat to 375°. Drop in turkey and stir to separate meat; cook for 1 minute. With a slotted spoon or a strainer, scoop up turkey. Heat oil until it is very hot again; return turkey to hot oil and fry for 2 more minutes until it is golden brown. Remove turkey from oil and drain.

Empty all but 1 Tbsp oil from wok. Set the wok over high heat; stir chili pepper and Szechuan peppercorns in hot oil for 15 seconds. Add garlic leaves or scallions, turkey, and soy sauce mixture; stir and blend everything evenly. Transfer to a plate and serve at once. Serves 4 to 6.

四 SZECHUAN DUCK
川
鴨

Of all the duck dishes I have eaten, Szechuan Duck is my all time favorite—marinated in aromatic spices, steamed, then deep-fried until crispy and dark brown. It is very fragrant and flavorful, a very impressive party dish.

- 1 duck, about 4 lbs
- ½ Tbsp star anise
- 1 tsp salt
- 2 Tbsps Shao-sing wine, sake, or dry sherry
- 1 Tbsp Szechuan peppercorns
- 8 slices of fresh ginger
- 5 scallions, cut into 2-inch sections
- 3 Tbsps soy sauce
- 1 tsp sugar
- 1 tsp five-spice powder
- 1 Tbsp cornstarch
- 6 cups oil
-    Szechuan peppercorn salt (see page 40)

Wash duck with cold water and dry thoroughly inside and out with paper towels. Remove the tip and the center part of the wings. Push the meat around the drumstick halfway up, then break and remove part of the drumstick bones. Place duck on a flat surface and press down on the breastbone with hands or pound it flat with the dull side of a cleaver (this step is optional).

Crush star anise with mortar and pestle.

Rub duck inside and out with salt and wine. Place peppercorns, star anise, ginger, and scallions inside and on top of the whole duck. Cover and marinate for 8 hours or overnight in the refrigerator.

Mix 2 Tbsps soy sauce and the sugar and five-spice powder together and coat inside and out of duck with the mixture.

Place duck in a large pan over boiling water, cover tightly, and steam over high heat for 2 hours. Drain off the juice from duck and remove ginger, scallions, peppercorns, and star anise. Let cool and dry for at least 2 hours. This step may be done a day in advance and stored in the refrigerator.

Coat duck with the remaining 1 Tbsp soy sauce and sprinkle cornstarch over duck. Pour oil into wok. Heat until very hot and fry duck until crisp and brown. The duck can be cut up into halves or into quarters before deep-drying. Chop duck into 1-inch pieces according to instructions on page 13, and arrange them neatly on a serving platter. Serves 6 to 8.

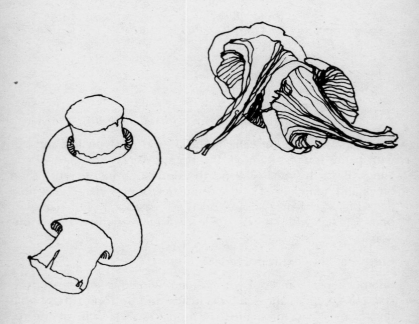

樟茶鴨 SMOKED CAMPHORWOOD TEA DUCK OR GOOSE

This celebrated duck dish is a superb example of the haute cuisine of Szechuan Province, rich in carefully contrasted flavors without the typical Szechuan spiciness. The name of the dish comes from its unique blending of flavors by smoking the duck with camphorwood chips and tea. In this recipe I substituted the spices for camphorwood chips.

> 1 duck about 5 lbs, or 1 goose about 8 lbs
> 2 tsps saltpeter
> 2 Tbsps warm water
> 3 Tbsps salt (5 Tbsps for goose)
> ½ Tbsp sugar (1 Tbsp for goose)
> 1 Tbsp Szechuan peppercorns (2 Tbsps for goose)
> 2 Tbsps Shao-sing wine, sake, or dry sherry (3 Tbsps for goose)
> 1 Tbsp crushed star anise
> 1 Tbsp black tea leaves
> 2 cinnamon sticks, crushed into small pieces
> ½ cup raw rice
> ½ cup brown sugar
> 5 cups of oil
> Szechuan peppercorn salt (see page 40)

Wash duck or goose inside and out under cold running water, and drain. Cut off the neck skin and remove excess fat. Dry inside and out thoroughly with paper towels.

In a small bowl dissolve saltpeter with the warm water. Pour half of the saltpeter solution into the cavity of the duck or goose and the rest over the body. Combine salt and sugar with ½ of the Szechuan peppercorns and rub the bird with the mixture inside and out. Marinate for 12 to 20 hours in the refrigerator.

Place bird on a large plate and set the plate on a rack in a large pan over boiling water. Cover tightly and steam over high heat for 1 hour according to instructions on page 21. Drain off the juice from bird and let cool and dry, about 6 hours or overnight. Smoke according to instructions on page 19, by placing the remaining Szechuan peppercorns and the star anise, tea, and cinnamon sticks on the bottom, then the rice on top of them. Lastly, sprinkle brown sugar on top of the rice. Smoke for 15 minutes. All this can be done a day in advance.

Just before serving, heat oil in a wok or deep-fryer over high heat. When oil is hot, lower duck or goose into oil and deep-fry until the skin is crisp. The bird can be cut up into 4 quarters before deep-frying. Remove bird from oil and drain. Chop into 1-inch by 2-inch pieces according to instructions on page 13 on how to cut up cooked poultry. Serve with Szechuan peppercorn salt. Serves 6 to 8.

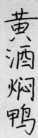

BRAISED DUCK IN WINE

1 duck, 4 to 5 lbs
¼ cup soy sauce
½ cup oil
1 cup Shao-sing wine or sake (no other substitute)
8 scallions, cut into 3-inch lengths
3 slices of ginger, about 1 inch in diameter
    Dash white pepper
1 cup water
1 tsp sugar
½ Tbsp cornstarch dissolved in 2 Tbsps water

Rinse duck and remove any fat. Dry thoroughly inside and out with paper towels. Coat outside of duck with 1 Tbsp soy sauce.

Heat oil in a wok over moderate heat until smoking. Brown duck in oil, making a quarter-turn every 2 minutes until the entire duck becomes golden brown. (Wear a long-sleeved outfit and rubber gloves to protect your arms and hands from the splattering oil.)

Place duck in a large pan; add wine, scallions, ginger, pepper, 1 cup water, and the remaining 3 Tbsps soy sauce. Cover and simmer for 1½ hours over low heat.

Transfer duck to a serving platter. Add sugar to stock and thicken with dissolved cornstarch. Pour sauce over duck and serve. This dish can be prepared in advance and reheated. Serves 4.

油 FRIED DUCK WITH
淋 SWEET AND SOUR
鸭 SAUCE DIP

This elegant party dish will certainly bring you applause. Tender, moist, and wonderfully flavored, it is simply delightful. Chicken can be substituted for the duck. I sometimes prepare a Peking duck (see page 140) and serve it in the same manner as this dish to avoid the deep-frying step.

   1 *duck, about 4 to 5 lbs*
 12 *cups water*
   2 *Tbsps Shao-sing wine, sake, or dry sherry*
   2 *scallions, each cut into 3 equal sections*
   3 *slices of ginger, 1 inch in diameter*
 ¼ *cup Chinese maltose syrup or corn syrup*
   4 *cups oil*
   1 *tsp minced ginger*
   2 *Tbsps finely chopped scallion*
   2 *Tbsps hoisin sauce*
 ½ *Tbsp soy sauce*
1½ *Tbsps cider vinegar*
   3 *Tbsps water*

Remove fat from duck and rinse inside and out thoroughly. In a large saucepan bring water, wine, scallion sections, ginger slices, and syrup to a boil; stir to dissolve the syrup. Put duck into the stock, breast-side down; bring to a boil. Cover pan, reduce heat to low, and simmer the duck for 30 minutes; turn duck over on its back and simmer for 30 more minutes. Remove duck from stock and place it on a cake rack to cool. Put the duck in the refrigerator on a few layers of paper towels without covering it, and let dry for 24 hours.

In a small pan heat 1 Tbsp oil over low heat until hot; stir in minced ginger and chopped scallion and cook for 20 seconds. Add hoisin sauce, soy sauce, vinegar, and 3 Tbsps water; simmer for 2 minutes.

Heat the remaining oil in a wok or a deep-fryer until hot, about 370°. Gently lower the duck into the oil and fry until the skin becomes golden brown. The duck can be cut up into quarters before deep-frying. Remove duck from oil and drain.

Cut the whole duck up into bite-sized pieces according to instructions on page 13. Place the pieces on a serving platter and pour the sauce over. Serve at once. Serves 8.

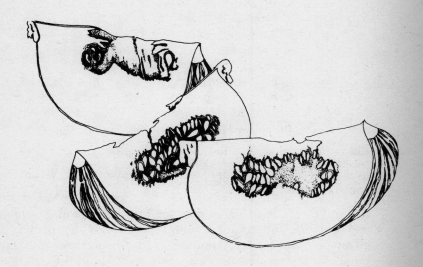

酸椒炒 STIR-FRIED GOOSE GIBLETS WITH PICKLED PEPPERS

Traditionally, goose intestines are included in this recipe along with the rest of the innards to make a substantial dish. Since American supermarkets do not sell poultry intestines, add more giblets of other birds to the dish when a large amount is needed. Turkey giblets work well with this recipe.

    1   set goose giblets (gizzard, liver, and heart)
    ½   Tbsp Shao-sing wine, sake, or dry sherry
    1   Tbsp soy sauce
    ¼   tsp sugar
    1   tsp sesame oil
    1   tsp cornstarch
    2   Tbsps chicken stock (see page 23)
    2   Tbsps oil
    1   tsp minced garlic
    1   tsp minced ginger
    ¼   cup shredded scallions
    ½   cup pickled peppers, cut into 1-inch squares

Cut the gizzard, liver, and heart into thin pieces.

In a small bowl, combine wine, soy sauce, sugar, sesame oil, cornstarch, and stock.

Heat oil in a wok or skillet over high heat; stir in garlic, ginger, and scallions and cook for about 15 seconds. Drop in goose giblets and stir-fry for 1 minute. Add mixture from the small bowl and the pickled peppers; stir and cook until the sauce is thickened. Transfer to a plate and serve at once. Serves 2 to 4.

酸
辣
汤
HOT AND SOUR SOUP

This thick, hearty soup is quick to assemble. The ingredients create an interesting contrast of textures. The full body of the soup makes a very satisfying light meal and is the perfect soup for cold weather.

     6 dried Chinese mushrooms, 2 inches in diameter
     ⅔ cup hot water
     ¼ lb boned chicken breast
     ½ Tbsp Shao-sing wine or sake
     2 Tbsps soy sauce
     ½ Tbsp cornstarch
     2 Tbsps water
4 to 5 cups canned or homemade chicken stock (see page 23)
     ½ cup bamboo shoots, cut into thin slivers
     1 square fresh bean curd, cut into 2-inch-long thin strips
     ½ tsp salt (omit salt if canned chicken stock is used)
     2 Tbsps cornstarch mixed with 3 Tbsps of water
     3 Tbsps white or cider vinegar
     ½ tsp white pepper (more or less according to taste)
     1 egg, beaten
     1 tsp sesame seed oil (optional)
     1 Tbsp minced scallion (optional)

Soak mushrooms in the hot water for 15 minutes; remove stems, then cut caps into thin slivers.

Cut chicken into 2-inch-long thin slivers. In a bowl mix chicken with wine, 1 Tbsp soy sauce, the cornstarch, and 2 Tbsps water. Set aside.

Over moderate heat, bring stock to a boil in a heavy saucepan.

Add chicken, mushrooms, and bamboo shoots and bring to a boil. Boil for about 1 minute.

Drop in bean curd, add the remaining soy sauce and salt, and bring soup to a boil again. Thicken the soup with dissolved cornstarch. Simmer for 30 seconds, then stir in vinegar and pepper.

Remove soup from heat and slowly stir in the beaten egg. When the egg is set, pour soup into a big serving bowl, add sesame seed oil, and garnish with minced scallion. Serve at once. This soup can be prepared in advance and reheated. Serves 6 to 8.

CHICKEN LIVER CUSTARD SOUP

鸡
肝
羊
、、、
汤

This is a very delicate banquet soup. Unlike other Szechuan dishes, which are spicy with a strong flavor, this dish is mild and subtle but rich. Since Chinese kitchens generally are not equipped with electric mixers and food processors, Chinese cooks have to spend hours pureeing the livers and preparing the broth. If you own a mixer or a food processor, it will take only a few minutes to complete this elegant dish.

10 oz chicken livers
4 cups chicken stock, canned or homemade (see page 23)
3 slices of ginger, crushed
2 scallions, pounded or crushed and cut into 2-inch sections
3 egg whites, slightly beaten
1 Tbsp Shao-sing wine, sake, or dry sherry
¾ tsp salt
Dash white pepper

Rinse chicken livers thoroughly and drain. Cut them into cubes; with a cleaver chop and puree them. Scoop the chicken livers into an mixing bowl and stir in 1½ cups cold chicken stock and the ginger, scallions, and egg whites. Or, put chicken liver cubes into an electric mixer or food processor, add 1½ cups cold chicken stock, and process until livers become a paste. Stir in ginger, scallions, and egg whites. (Do not process the mixture as it must not become foamy.)

Strain liver mixture into another mixing bowl; stir in wine, ¼ tsp salt, and the pepper. Pour into a soup tureen or into six individual soup bowls. Place the bowl or bowls in a steamer over boiling water and partially cover. According to instructions on page

21, steam the liver custards over low heat until set (about 25 minutes for a large bowl and 15 minutes for small bowls).

In a small saucepan, bring the remaining chicken stock to a boil and season with the remaining salt, more or less according to taste. Gently pour the stock into the liver custard or custards and serve. Serves 6 to 8.

汽锅鸡 YUNNAN DISTILLED CHICKEN SOUP

This special steamed chicken soup is a deluxe version of ordinary chicken soup. Its unique feature is the Yunnan pot in which the broth is prepared—a round clay pot with a funnel built right in the center sprouting up all the way from the base to the top and tapered into a small opening. Pieces of chicken are placed around the funnel along with other ingredients, then the pot is covered with a lid and put inside a pan, which should be a few inches wider and taller than the clay pot. When the water in the outside pan is boiling, the steam rises through the funnel and condenses into water when it hits the lid. This provides the finished dish with the right amount of pure, rich, and flavorful broth. Meanwhile, the chicken is being cooked by the surrounding boiling water and the steam that comes through the hole. Yunnan pots can be ordered or bought at Oriental grocery stores. A lidded casserole can be used in place of the Yunnan pot.

> 2 lbs chicken, all legs, or ½ chicken breast and ½
>   chicken legs
> 2 scallions, cut into 2-inch sections
> 4 slices of ginger, about 1 inch in diameter
> 1 Tbsp Shao-sing wine, sake, or dry sherry
> 2 cups chicken stock (see page 23) or water
>   Salt to taste

Disjoint the chicken legs; cut each thigh and drumstick crosswise into 2 pieces. If chicken breast is used, split the whole breast lengthwise into 2 halves, then cut each half crosswise into 3 or 4 pieces. Place chicken into the Yunnan pot; add scallions, ginger, wine, and stock or water. Cover with the lid, put the pot into a large pan on a top of a cake rack. Fill the outside pan with boiling water to come to about midway up the Yunnan pot. Cover the outside pan and steam over high heat for 2 hours. Replenish with more boiling water every half hour or 45 minutes.

Remove clay pot from the large pan, uncover, and discard ginger and scallions. Season with salt and serve. Serves 6 to 8.

Note: For variation, 6 to 8 soaked Chinese black mushrooms may be added to the pot with the raw chicken. Soak black mushrooms in 1 cup hot water for 30 minutes. Remove stems and add the caps to soup.

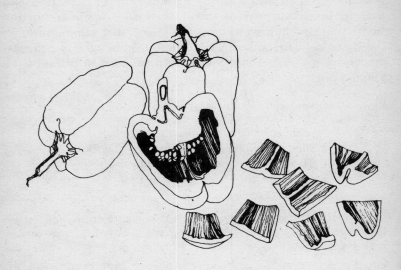

CHICKEN AND SZECHUAN PRESERVED VEGETABLE SOUP

搾菜鸡片汤

This is a delicate yet flavorful soup appropriate for any season and every occasion. The Szechuan preserved vegetable adds just a hint of spiciness for an exciting taste.

> 2 oz Szechuan preserved vegetable
> 6 oz boned chicken breast
> 1 tsp cornstarch
> ½ Tbsp light soy sauce
> 1 Tbsp oil
> 2 Tbsps finely chopped scallion
> 3 cups chicken stock, canned or homemade (see page 23)
> Salt to taste (optional)

Rinse off the pepper coating from the Szechuan preserved vegetable, then cut into thin slivers.

Following the instructions on page 16, cut chicken into thin slices and then into slivers, mix chicken with cornstarch and soy sauce.

In a saucepan heat oil over medium heat, then stir in scallion and cook for 30 seconds or until some pieces become light brown. Add stock and Szechuan preserved vegetable; cover pan and simmer over low heat for 10 minutes.

Uncover pan, add chicken, and bring soup to a boil. Remove from heat and serve. Add salt if desired. Serves 4.

MAIL ORDER SOURCES
FOR CHINESE INGREDIENTS

The following list of Chinese grocery stores is for the convenience of those who live in areas that have no Oriental shops. All the stores listed here carry most of the ingredients and different types of poultry that are called for in the recipes in this book and will handle mail orders.

ATLANTA
Chinatown Store, 2743 La Vista Road NE, Atlanta, Georgia 30329

BOSTON
Sun Chong Lung Co., 50 Beach Street, Boston, Massachusetts 02111

CHICAGO
Star Market, 3349 North Clark Street, Chicago, Illinois 60657

FLORIDA
Wild Oak Plantation, P.O. Box 2405, Jacksonville, Florida 32203 (Poultry only)

LOS ANGELES
Wing Chong Lung Co., 922 San Pedro Street, Los Angeles, California 90015

MINNEAPOLIS
Asia Mart, 908 Marquette Ave., Minneapolis, Minnesota 55402

NEW YORK
East Wind, 2801 Broadway, New York, New York 10025
Kam Man Food Products, Inc., 200 Canal Street, New York, New York 10013
Liang's Oriental Gifts and Grocery, Inc., 17 Saw Hill River Road (Route 9A), Elmsford, New York 10523

PHILADELPHIA

Joy Dragon Food Market, 1022 Race Street, Philadelphia,
  Pennsylvania 19107

SAN FRANCISCO

The Chinese Grocer, 209 Post Street, San Francisco, California
  94108

Lin Trading Co., 118 Stockton Street, San Francisco, California
  94133

Metro Food Co., 641 Broadway, San Francisco, California
  94133

Irving Enterprises, Inc., 681 Broadway, San Francisco, California
  94133

Wo Soon Produce Co., 1210 Stockton Street, San Francisco,
  California 94133

SEATTLE

Foodway Super Market and Kitchen, 2000 South Jackson Street,
  Seattle, Washington 98144

WASHINGTON, D.C.

Shu Ling Co., 672 North Glebe Road, Arlington, Virginia 22203

CANADA

QUEBEC

Arando Hasimoto, RR I, Thurso, Quebec Province JOX3BO
  (Poultry only)

TORONTO

Wing Fong Trading Co., 136 Dundas Street West, Toronto,
  Canada MSG 1C3

VANCOUVER

Wing Hing Co., Ltd., 280 East Pender Street, Vancouver, Canada
  V6A 1T7

INDEX